Lord of the Sky

DORIS GATES

LORD OF THE SKY Zeus

Illustrated by Robert Handville

The Viking Press   *New York*

First published in 1972 by The Viking Press, Inc.
625 Madison Avenue, New York, N.Y. 10022
Published simultaneously in Canada by
The Macmillan Company of Canada Limited
Library of Congress catalog card number: 72–80514
Printed in U.S.A.
398   1. Zeus
      2. Greek Myths
SBN 670-44051-5
2 3 4 5 76 75

*These stories are all dedicated to
the boys and girls of
Fresno County, California,
who heard them first*

CONTENTS

Zeus
and Hera

All-High, they called him: Zeus, father of gods and of men. His power was vast as the sky, mighty as the roll of thunder, and his moods as swift-changing as the clouds that swept the slopes of high Mount Olympus, home of the gods.

Their great palaces were scattered all up and down the mist-shrouded slopes of the mighty mountain. Pillars of ivory and cornices of gold sparkled with dazzling brilliance when the sun's rays pierced the mists and made them shimmer with all the glory of light on snow. No mortals had ever penetrated to these heights. Guarding their flocks in the green meadows below, men lifted their eyes to the summits above them, speculating on the wonders which they surely knew must lie hidden behind the drifting cloud banks.

Zeus, lord of the sky, had for his wife the goddess Hera.

She was one of the three most important goddesses on Olympus and, as wife of Zeus, could command the respect of gods and men alike, though she did not always deserve it. For Hera was a jealous wife. Though Zeus gave her cause for jealousy, a jealous wife, even when she is a goddess, is an object of scorn.

Once, enraged by her husband's unfaithfulness, she decided to punish him. Putting her plan before Poseidon and Athena, who had their own reasons for wanting to see Zeus overthrown, she persuaded them to bind him while he slept. Then they were to hurl him out of heaven.

The plot might have succeeded if Thetis, a sea nymph, had not heard of it. She left her deep sea cavern and sped away to summon help for Zeus. It came in the form of a giant with a hundred hands and fifty heads. This monster had only to seat himself beside the sleeping Zeus to prevent anyone approaching him, for no one dared to provoke the monster's wrath.

When Zeus learned of the plot (for nothing could be concealed from him), he clapped golden handcuffs onto Hera's wrists and hung her from the top of the sky. And there she stayed with a golden anvil dragging at her heels until she agreed not to plot another woe against her husband. When you plot against a god, you must be certain you destroy him!

From this time on, Hera's jealous rages were directed against the unlucky objects of her husband's romantic attentions.

One of the most hapless among these maidens was Io.

The
Story of Io

Io was one of the most beautiful maidens in all Greece, the pride of her father's house. No flower in all the flower-filled meadows through which she drove her father's flocks could match the quiet beauty of her face. Her brown eyes, wide with wonder, were gentle as a heifer's, and her slim body moved with the grace of tall reeds leaning in the wind.

One day Zeus, looking down upon Earth from high Olympus, let his idle gaze wander to the sunny meadow where Io was tending her flocks. Instantly his eye was caught by the graceful figure of the girl walking there. Never had he beheld a mortal maiden so comely. And, since Zeus could seldom resist the charms of mortal maidens, in another moment he had fallen hopelessly in love with Io.

He descended at once to Earth and approached the girl. But she, seeing the shining form of the god, took fright and fled. At this, Zeus caused a heavy cloud to form about her so that Io could not see to run and so was forced to stay and listen to the god's pleadings.

"Do not be afraid," he said. "This is a god who stands before you—and no ordinary god. I am Zeus, hurler of thunderbolts, who now declares his love for you."

While Zeus wooed Io in the misty meadow, Hera, suddenly aware of her husband's absence, began searching for him throughout Olympus. Not finding him there, she cast her eyes upon Earth and was startled to see a well-defined area of fog at the edge of a sunny meadow. Since there was no fog anywhere else, Hera's suspicions were aroused.

Gathering her robes about her, she descended rapidly to the very spot where the mist lay thick upon the ground.

"I may be mistaken," she said to herself, "but I believe my husband is doing me great wrong."

She set about breaking up the cloud.

But Zeus, from whom nothing could be concealed, already knew that his wife was looking for him. Before she could quite clear the mist away, he had changed Io into a beautiful white heifer, with soft dark eyes. So when at last Hera was able to see what lay before her, she saw only her husband standing in a flowery meadow, his hand resting lightly upon the back of a lovely heifer. Even Hera's hate-filled heart softened as she looked upon the gentle creature.

"Where did you get this heifer?" she demanded. "And where are her other comrades of the herd?" Hera's suspicions were by no means quieted. No earthly kine had ever possessed such beauty!

"Just now, before my very eyes, she sprang from the earth as you see her," lied Zeus.

Hera smiled cruelly, not believing a word he said.

"Then if she is sprung from Earth, could I not have her as a present?"

Zeus hesitated. He loved Io and could not bear to surrender her into Hera's hands. Yet he very well knew that if he did not yield her up, Hera would surely become more certain that this was no heifer after all. To withhold such a small gift would only betray its real importance. Reluctantly, Zeus gave Io, in the form of a heifer, into Hera's keeping.

Hera, still suspicious, placed the lovely heifer under the guard of Argus, a monster with a hundred eyes, only two of which ever closed in slumber—all the rest kept watch. No matter which way he faced, no matter where he stood or sat, he was at all times looking at Io. She was never out of his sight. During the day Argus permitted her to graze like any ordinary heifer, but at night he tied her in a cave and sat at its mouth to prevent anyone entering.

Io's sufferings were as pitiful as they were cruel. She knew she had been changed from human form. When she opened her mouth to lament her fate, a gentle lowing was all the sound she could make. Her heart was near breaking with the awful injustice.

One day as she was grazing across a familiar meadow, she came to the stream that flowed near her father's house. With joy she splashed across it and ran toward her home. But no one knew her when she came there, neither her sisters nor her father. Delighted with her beauty, they petted her and pulled sweet grasses for her. Vainly Io tried to tell them who she was, but always her voice came forth as a gentle lowing. At last a happy thought came to her, and, raising a front hoof, she scratched in the dust before them the letter *I*. Next she added an *O*, then looked imploringly at her family, her gentle eyes beseeching them to understand what she was trying to tell them. Suddenly her father knew her and flung his arms around her snowy neck, crying out, "Ah, what miserable fortune is this which has come upon us. I have sought you far and wide, my daughter, but never did I dream of such a fate for you as this." Before he could say more, Argus, the hundred-eyed, arrived and drove the heifer away.

However, Zeus, sitting on a mountaintop above the meadow, had seen it all, and his selfish heart was moved with deep pity for poor Io. He sought out his son Hermes, the messenger of the gods, and bade him kill Argus. It was a difficult task, but Hermes had two properties at hand to help him: his winged sandals, which bore him swiftly through the air; and his wand, which gave him the power to make anyone fall asleep. When he had equipped himself with these aids, Hermes mounted into the air to begin a search for Argus. He raced along the sky, leaping and skipping for the sheer joy of knowing himself borne aloft by his winged sandals. At last, near the edge of a meadow reaching up onto a hillside where a grove of oak trees clustered, Hermes found the monster Argus. A snow-white heifer was grazing near him.

Hermes removed his sandals, and reaching into a leather pouch which swung from his shoulder, he took out a little pipe of reeds. He began to play a merry tune, and soon some inquisitive goats, caught by the music, came forth from a clump of bushes. Driving these before him and still playing on his pipe, Hermes, appearing for all the world like a simple goatherd, slowly crossed the meadow in the direction of Argus.

As soon as Argus heard the music, he rose and called to Hermes to come and join him on his rock in the shade.

"Come and sit beside me, young goatherd," Argus invited. And the white heifer raised her head and with mournful eyes watched the approach of the young god across the grass.

So Hermes and Argus sat together chatting. Every once in a while, Hermes played a melody upon his pipe, and, when he did, Argus had great difficulty in keeping his ninety-eight unsleeping eyes open. At length, to fend off sleep the monster begged his visitor to explain how he had come by his pipe of reeds. "For never in all my wanderings have I ever seen anything like it, nor have I ever heard music so sweet," declared Argus.

And Hermes, pleased at the request, began with his nimble tongue to relate the story of Syrinx.

Once upon a time on the mountain slopes of Arcadia

there lived a wood nymph by the name of Syrinx. She had many suitors, for she was a pretty young girl. But she refused to choose one from among them and avoided them all, for she had taken vows to live alone and free like Artemis, goddess of the hunt and protector of all wild things.

Now one day the great god Pan beheld Syrinx as she glided among the forest trees, and he fell in love with her. When she refused to listen to his pleas, but fled from him instead, he pursued her and was about to overtake her as they came to the edge of a river. Here the frightened and desperate nymph begged the river nymphs to take pity on her and change her into some other form. This they gladly and quickly did. Suddenly there sprang up on the riverbank tall reeds, which made a gentle music as the wind stirred them. Pan, sorrowing, put forth his arms and gathered the reeds into them.

"At least I shall have these," he cried.

He took the reeds and bound them together in such a way that when he blew upon them pleasant and varying tones were given off. He called this new pipe a syrinx after the maiden he had loved. Ever after Pan—half goat, half man—has played upon a reed instrument, which in some regions is known as the Pipes of Pan.

As Hermes ended his tale, he saw that all the eyes of Argus were closed, his head nodding. Quickly, the god seized his wand and struck the monster with it just where his head joined his shoulders. Thus was his slumber deepened. Taking a curved blade from his pouch, Hermes struck off the head of Argus.

Io was now free of her fearful guardian, but she was by no means free of Hera and her wrath. For the wife of Zeus was certain now that her lovely heifer was no ordinary creature, but a maiden whom her guilty husband had tried to conceal from her. Hera's jealousy was a raging fire within her, consuming all compassion in an urge to make Io suffer even greater torment. To this end, Hera sent a gadfly to sting the heifer ceaselessly. Tortured past endurance, the poor creature ran from meadow to mountain and from mountain to sea, hoping always to rid herself of the persistent pest. One sea she crossed has ever after borne her name, the Ionian Sea. Throughout all the world she roamed even to the highest peaks of the mighty Caucasus Mountains, which divide Europe from Asia. Here she came upon a dreadful sight, a man, a living man, bound to a great granite rock by iron shackles. Io stopped, aghast.

"Who are you," she lowed, "whose sufferings are a match for mine. What have you done to deserve such punishment?"

Reading her thought, the man answered, "I am Prometheus, the Titan who gave fire to mankind. Zeus had forbidden it to them, but I stole it from heaven and gave it to man to make him great. And so Zeus has punished me."

It was Prometheus who had established the race of men

upon Earth. Taking clay from a riverbank, he had artfully molded it into the likeness of the gods. Then a friend of his among the Immortals, the goddess Athena, had breathed life into his creation. The men of clay became men of flesh, moving with the purpose of the living. Yet they were only half alive. They still did not know how to employ their bodies' strength or how to direct their spirits. They moved about on the earth in aimless wanderings, and, like the animals, they made their homes in caves.

Prometheus, taking pity upon these creatures of his creating, began to instruct them. First he made them aware of the stars and the moon and the changing seasons. He taught them how to harness animals and use their strength to lighten the tasks of field and forest. He showed them how to use herbs to cure illnesses, and he added to their comfort in many other ways. One thing alone he could not give them—fire. Zeus controlled that mighty force.

Now Zeus, when he became aware of what was going on, took a hostile view of Prometheus's activities. The Father of Gods disliked the idea of another race inhabiting the earth which, until now, had been the province of the gods alone. He was angry at what Prometheus had done and expressed his wrath by withholding the gift of fire from man. Zeus well knew that in refusing to give fire to man, he could curb this new and puny creature that was without fangs or claws for his protection or fur to cover him. Let him keep such gifts as Prometheus had given him. What harm could man direct against the gods without the gift of fire?

But Prometheus was crafty as well as inventive. Moreover, it gave him pleasure to defy all-powerful Zeus whose ruthless selfishness was making life difficult for men. Breaking off a stalk of fennel, he carried it high in the heavens, where the chariot of the sun would pass at midday. When the fiery chariot blazed across the heavens, Prometheus thrust the stalk of fennel between the spokes of a wheel. A bright flame spurted up and traveled back inside the fennel, along the pithy part of the stalk where it could safely smolder. Straightway Prometheus descended to Earth and gave the burning stalk to man. Soon the first brush fire was sending its smoke to heaven, and thankful mortals were gathering around it, warming their cold bodies against its wall of heat.

Zeus, instantly aware of what had happened, felt a powerful rage. Prometheus must be punished and most terribly. And so Zeus had him seized and bound and carried to this bleak mountain in the Caucasus, where he was shackled in irons to endure the heat of day and the frost of night. And suffer torment greater yet.

Hardly had Prometheus finished his sad speech to Io, when she heard the rush of huge wings, and an eagle settled on the rock beside Prometheus and began to tear at his liver. The sky shook with Prometheus's screams, but the eagle continued its grisly feasting. When it had finished, it flew away, and the god's liver grew back again as it had been before.

"Thus am I tortured each day." Prometheus told the sorrowing Io. "And thus shall I continue to suffer until

great Heracles shall come to set me free. And mankind, too, has not escaped the wrath of Zeus."

While Io listened, Prometheus told of the vengeance Zeus had taken upon man for his possession of fire. Now that he had it, not even Zeus could take the stolen gift away, but Zeus would see to it that man throughout all eternity paid for the gift.

Up to the time he stole the fire from heaven, Prometheus told her, only men were to be found on earth. Women had not come among them yet, but now Zeus saw a way to take revenge. He ordered his son Hephaestus, who was god of the forge, to fashion a figure in the shape of a woman. She must have the beauty of a goddess but not the chilling dignity and sternness of a goddess. Her smile must be sweet and winning and her eyes and lips warm. All her form and features should be beguiling, irresistible to the eyes of man. So Hephaestus went to work, and when he had finished, the figure he presented to Zeus was so lovely that it excited the admiration of all the gods and goddesses. They each bestowed a gift upon the lovely thing, and then Hermes led her down to Earth and presented her to Epimetheus, brother of Prometheus.

"Here," said Hermes, "is Pandora, whom Zeus has sent to be your wife."

Prometheus had many times warned his brother never to accept a gift from the ruler of Olympus. But when Epimetheus gazed upon the beauty of Pandora, he forgot his brother's warning and gladly welcomed his new wife. Then he saw that she carried in her arms a beautiful box, richly wrought and set with precious stones. Its lid was closed.

"How did you come by such a beautiful thing?" Epimetheus asked her.

"Zeus placed it in my hands as I departed Olympus," she told him.

"And what does it hold?" Epimetheus asked.

"I do not know; the Father of Gods told me never to inquire and never to lift the lid."

"Then," declared Epimetheus, "we shall admire its beauty and not seek to know more about it."

But as the days passed, Pandora's curiosity about the jeweled box grew and grew. At last it consumed her utterly, and she knew that she could no longer endure not to know what it contained.

She waited until one day when Epimetheus left the house. She quickly hurried to where the box sat and lifted its lid. A furious buzzing sounded suddenly, and then a cloud dark as smoke circled up from the opened box as millions of insect-like creatures flew forth. These were the plagues, which until now the earth had never known. Pandora, blinded by the sudden swarm, struggled to put back the lid. By the time she managed it, all the anxieties, misfortunes, and bad luck which plague mankind had flown out of the house and into every corner of the world. One thing only remained inside the box: hope.

"So man has fire, and endless misfortune—and hope." Prometheus told Io. "And here am I because of my love

for man. And here I must stay, still defying Zeus until one greater than he shall set me free."

His head fell forward upon his breast, and Io, driven again by the gadfly, continued her lonely, aimless wanderings, her heart filled with sorrow for the god who had dared so much in order to help the race of man.

She came at last to the waters of the Nile, and here she stopped. She could endure no more, and, kneeling beside the stream, she lifted her cow's head to heaven. Lowing helplessly, she begged Zeus to free her from her torments. Seeing her thus, the god was moved. He went to Hera and confessed everything and pleaded with her to end Io's sufferings.

"I swear by the river Styx that you will never again have anything to fear from Io," promised Zeus.

Hera could not fail to be impressed by this oath. The Styx was the river of the lower world that carried the souls of the dead to their final resting place. No god could swear by the Styx and go against his oath. So Hera knew she no longer would need to be jealous of Io. Her anger against the maiden gradually lessened and at last disappeared altogether.

Io became what she had been before, a gentle maiden blessed with beauty and a voice clear, pleasing, and, above all, human.

Deucalion's Flood

Despite the troubles Pandora loosed upon the world, shortly after her arrival on Earth, mankind entered upon an Age of Gold. It was a blessed time. People walked without fear and lived easily. There was neither heat nor cold and all things grew in abundance.

But the Age of Gold passed into the Age of Silver when the seasons came to divide the year, and man knew again the cold of winter and the harsh heat of summer. No longer could he wander as he willed. Permanent shelter was required, and with it came a need to plow a living from the land.

Then came the Age of Bronze, and man learned how to hate his neighbor and to avenge his wrongs with war.

Finally there came the Age of Iron. Now all men were

seized with a great urge to *have*. They swept the mountains bare of trees to make their ships. They dug into the
earth to seek its precious metals. Land once free to all became the property of the one who could defend it. And
everywhere in this frenzied pursuit of things, men forgot
the gods. No smoke of incense rose from honored altars.
Nowhere were the gods appeased or thanked, though
often they were cursed.

Zeus had for some time been aware of the spreading ar-
rogance and greed among mortals. When at last they began to defy the gods, his anger reached a climax. One
night, disguised as an ordinary traveler, he descended to
Earth and approached a splendid palace where a feast was
in progress. Lights shown forth brilliantly from behind
its stately columns, and the sound of music met the god
as he crossed the paved terrace. Fearlessly he strode toward
the great hall, but a guard rudely stopped him at the
entrance.

"Fool," he said, "do you not know that this is the palace
of Lycaon? Who are you to force an entrance here?"

Angered at this inhospitable speech to a weary traveler,
Zeus replied, "I am come from Olympus and I demand
the honor due to gods, if not to strangers, in this house."

He spoke boldly and Lycaon heard his words. So did
all his guests. Some of them, noting the awful fire in the
stranger's eye and the fearful dignity of his bearing, began
to offer up prayers. But Lycaon laughed at their pious
gestures.

"How do you know this fellow is a god?" he sneered.

"You have but his word for it. However, I know a way to prove his immortality." He laughed coldly. "Stay with us this night, stranger, and by morning it shall be proved whether or not you are what you claim to be."

It was all too clear to Zeus that Lycaon meant to kill him while he slept, and his wrath grew at the brutality of the plan. But there was even worse in Lycaon's heart. He ordered a hostage brought and had him killed upon the spot. Then he directed that parts of the victim's flesh be broiled and set before the hungry stranger. This was enough proof to Zeus of the depths to which mankind had sunk, and his wrath exploded. Revealing himself as a god, he struck his fist against the air, and a bolt of lightning flashed in the great hall.

Lycaon fled, howling. By the time he had reached some far-off fields, a great change had come upon him. Flecks of foam dropped from his mouth, which opened like a dog's to reveal great fangs and a bloody tongue. His sides became shaggy, and he fell upon all fours. He tried to speak but managed only a whimper that rose again to a howl. He had become a wolf and such he would remain. Thus Zeus had punished him for his cruelty.

But still the rest of mankind remained to be dealt with, for Zeus had seen enough to sicken his heart. This race must be destroyed, and quickly. At first Zeus thought to erase the earth with fire, but then he realized this might endanger the heavens where the gods dwelled. Better, he decided, to send a flood and drown the world.

In order to accomplish this, Zeus needed the help of

two gods: Aeolus, god of the winds; and Poseidon, god of the sea. He ordered Aeolus to shut in his cave the north wind and any other winds whose business it was to clear the sky of clouds. Then he told Aeolus to summon the south wind, and he came, his head wreathed in fog. Water dripped from his wings, which he spread across the sky, shutting out the sun and turning all the heavens into pitchy darkness. Out of this darkness, rain began to fall. It came upon the earth in endless torrents of water.

Meanwhile, Poseidon was rallying the power of all the rivers. Everywhere the waters rose and the land was flooded. The sea rose, too, as the rivers flung their waters into it. Where houses and temples had stood, there was only water. Fishes swam among the treetops, and wolves and lions and tigers swam among herds of sheep and goats. It was a sea without a shore, and men pulled on oars where once they had held the plow.

A few, a very few, people managed to climb to where now and then a hilltop rose above the surface of this swiftly summoned sea. But these soon starved to death, for nowhere was anything left that men could eat. All crops and animals were drowned.

At last there remained lifted above the raging waters only the twin peaks that crown the top of Mount Parnassus. And here two weary, frightened mortals took refuge. A man and a woman, the only people left on Earth. Deucalion was the man's name, and his wife was Pyrrah. These were good people, the man kind and just, the woman ever mindful of the gods and reverent toward them. Out of all the people who had inhabited the earth, these two alone were left alive.

Zeus saw them wet and cold and frightened as they clung to each other atop the mountain, and he remembered their blameless lives and their faithful worship. He was moved to compassion by their plight. Quickly, he ordered Aeolus to free the north wind that he might blow away the storm clouds. Next he signaled Poseidon, who, in his turn ordered his son Triton to sound a retreat to the waters. Triton rose from the ocean floor and heaved above its surface, his mighty shoulders dripping with sea water and studded with barnacles. Then with his huge hands he lifted to his lips a hollow shell and blew a piercing blast upon it. The sound waves of that sea horn traveled across the reaching waters, and the ocean heard and began withdrawing from the land. Tall trees began to appear upon the hillsides, their branches hung about with seaweed. Temples rose from the receding water, their marble columns slick with mud and slime. Down, down the water ran until the shoreline was again where it had been before. The sun shone forth and the land began to steam and finally to dry.

Deucalion and Pyrrah wept to see the earth returning to its former state. Their tears were partly for joy at their own deliverance, but partly because of their sorrow at the awful fate that had been visited upon all the rest of mankind.

"Dear wife," said Deucalion, "the only woman left on Earth as I am the only man, would that I possessed the power of my father, Prometheus, who fashioned man from clay. Then might I put another race upon this earth to plow its fields and make it fruitful again. How lonely is our lot, the only two people left on Earth! What would be your fate, Pyrrah, were I to die and leave you quite alone? And how will I face life if you die before me?" He sat for a time in deepest sorrow, as Pyrrah tried to comfort him with brave words. Finally, he lifted his head. He straightened and pointed down the mountain. "Look," he cried, "there is a temple below us. Let us go to it now and ask of the god or goddess whose spirit dwells there what we should do."

They rose and descended the mountain to where the temple stood. They entered its porch and slowly proceeded into the damp interior. All about them was the smell of salt and seaweed, but they approached the ruined altar which, they saw, was dedicated to Themis, an oracle. Reverently they threw themselves upon their knees before it.

"Great Themis," Deucalion prayed, "goddess of justice who sits beside Father Zeus upon the throne of heaven, mighty Themis, we give you thanks for sparing our poor lives. But how shall we manage now alone upon the earth? What is to become of us?"

A voice answered him from above the altar. "Go forth from this temple with your heads covered and your garments loosened. And cast behind you the bones of your mother.''

At these words, Deucalion and Pyrrah looked at each other with dismay.

"How can we obey the oracle?" asked Pyrrah. "We dare not disturb the remains of our parents!"

They waited, but the oracle did not speak again, and quietly the pair left the temple. They walked to a little grove of trees, and here they sat themselves to consider what the words might mean.

After a long silence, Deucalion spoke. "The gods never ask us to do wrong. That command must be something we can obey without offense to the dead." He thought a minute. Suddenly his face lit. "I have it, Pyrrah. The earth is our mother; the stones are her bones. Let us gather some at once and cast them behind us. If I am wrong in thinking thus, at least it can do no harm. Let us try."

So they covered their heads, loosened their clothes, and, gathering an armful of stones each, they started to cast them over their shoulders. Instantly, a wonderful thing happened. As the stones fell to the ground, they began to turn soft and then to take on the shapes of men and women. The stones thrown by Deucalion became men; those which Pyrrah threw became women. The figures grew gradually, as a statue takes form from the rock a sculptor works with hammer and chisel. The moss and slime that had gathered on them from the flood became flesh. The hard stone formed their bones, and the veins that crisscrossed the rock became veins for carrying their life's blood.

And so a new race of men was placed upon the earth. A race ready for the tasks which lay ahead of it, a race as hard and durable as stone.

Baucis
and Philemon

Centuries passed. Men established themselves upon the earth, building cities, tilling the land, hunting in the forests, sailing upon the seas, living the lives that fate accorded them. Some were rich, some poor; some were kind and compassionate. Others were selfish and cruel, indifferent to human suffering.

Now in those times in Asia Minor there was a country known as Phrygia. Had you been a traveler in that ancient land, you would eventually have come upon a place where a marsh spread wide its reeds and shallow waters. You would have seen on a hilltop overlooking this marsh a temple white and columned, in front of which a strange tree was growing. Though its branches rose from a single trunk, one half of this tree was an oak and the other half was a linden.

In those times, as in the period before Deucalion's flood, Zeus often descended from Olympus to Earth in order to test its inhabitants. Were they faithful in their worship of the gods? Did justice prevail among them? Was the good and bad at least equally divided among them?

To find the answer to these questions, Zeus one day decided to visit Phrygia. He called Hermes to him, and disguising themselves as simple travelers, the two gods journeyed to Earth.

They came at last to a fair city that rose above a small plain backed by gentle hills. Rows of streets lined with handsome houses presented themselves to the gods.

Sweeping his eyes along the house fronts, the Father of Gods strode to the largest and struck its door with his fist. It was opened by a house slave, who looked haughtily at the two grimy travelers and demanded to know what they wished.

"We are weary and hungry," said Zeus, "and beg rest and food."

"We have nothing here for beggars," said the slave and slammed the door in the gods' faces.

They proceeded to the next house. And the next and the next. With each it was the same. Their owners had given orders not to assist a stranger. All through the city the two gods trudged, but no one took compassion on them, no one offered them hospitality. Such behavior angered Zeus, for he was the god of beggars and travelers, who must depend on the generosity of others.

Zeus and Hermes continued their quest until it led

them to the outskirts of the city, where the houses were no longer handsome and the streets no longer paved. Marching along in the dust, the two approached a tiny cabin with a roof made of reeds and a door which hung crookedly on leather straps. Zeus knocked, and the door opened slowly, scraping over a dirt floor.

An old woman peered out at the traveler on her doorstep and said in a faltering voice, "What do you wish of us, stranger?"

"We have traveled a long way," replied Zeus, "and we are tired and hungry."

The old woman stepped back. "Come in, come in," she said. "Of course, come in."

The door was so low that the gods had to stoop to enter. Once inside they were greeted by the old woman's husband, who rose to meet his guests.

"You are welcome here," he said. He placed a gentle hand on the old woman's shoulder. "This is my good wife Baucis, and I am Philemon. We have grown old together in this same cottage, and we have been content."

The old couple smiled at each other. Philemon pulled forward a rude bench and upon it Baucis spread a robe, which her gnarled fingers had woven. Philemon urged the gods to be seated, while Baucis bustled over to the little hearth where she began blowing on the ashes until a bright spark glowed. Then she broke twigs and pieces of bark and fed the fire. A blaze leaped up, and the little cabin became warm and cheerful in its light.

Next she put a copper kettle on the burning sticks and

filled it half full of water. Philemon brought a fresh fat cabbage from the garden behind the house and Baucis put it into the kettle. Bringing down a piece of bacon from the low rafters overhead, Philemon added this to the cabbage. All the while the two old people kept up a lively conversation with their visitors to pass the time before the hungry wanderers could eat.

When the meat and the cabbage were ready, and their good smell was filling the room, Philemon pulled a couch up to the rickety table. Baucis arranged a mattress stuffed with sweet, dried grass upon the couch and covered it with the finest cloth she owned, in honor of the strangers.

Zeus and Hermes took their places on the couch, reclining as best they could in accordance with the custom for dining in those days.

And now food was placed before the gods. It was served in heavy, coarse pottery bowls, crudely shaped. The mixing bowl for the wine was of the same quality, and the wine goblets set before the guests were made of wood and lined with wax.

But no word of apology passed the old couple's lips. This was what they had; this was the best they had. And they were proud and happy that they could put food before the travelers. Philemon served the wine with a flourish, though it was hardly better than vinegar and had water added to it.

Zeus and Hermes began to eat and drink, and their appetites were hearty. Never could anyone have guessed that they were used to better fare than this. The old couple watched them with delight and kept pressing more food and drink upon them. Besides the cabbage and bacon there were olives and cherries. There were radishes and cheese and eggs roasted in their shells in the hot ashes.

But all at once, Philemon became aware of something very strange. As often as he filled the wooden goblets, the amount of wine in the mixing bowl remained the same. Now Baucis had noticed, too, and with one frightened glance between them, they flung themselves on their knees, for well they knew that they were in the presence of gods.

"Forgive us this poor fare, unfit for gods," Philemon pleaded.

But Zeus, all-wise all-father answered him, "Any food is fit for gods when generously shared."

At this moment there came over the threshold of the little cabin a white goose that the old couple kept as a kind of watchdog and household pet. As Philemon's eye fell upon it, he knew what he must do to honor their guests. The goose must be sacrificed. To set a roast goose before these Immortals would restore the honor of their hosts and erase all memory of the lean and simple meal which had been first placed before them. Rising painfully from his knees, Philemon signaled to Baucis, who also struggled up and made for the unsuspecting goose. But it was too quick for the slow-moving old pair. Beating its wings so that the little cabin suddenly seemed filled with a cyclone, it flew over the table in the very faces of the gods. Zeus let out a roar of laughter in which Hermes joined.

The old couple seemed not to notice the gods' mirth in their earnest pursuit of the goose, which managed always to elude them. At last it flapped its way to the couch where the gods sat, and Zeus laid a hand on its white back.

"Spare your goose, good people," he told the breathless pair. "You have served us well and need add nothing to what you have given us. We are indeed gods, as you know. So now come with us to the mountaintop. This wicked city shall pay as it deserves for its hardheartedness. But you have no need for worry. Leave your house now and come with us."

Obedient to the god's command, each took a walking staff in hand and followed the gods up the steep slope of the mountain. They had climbed to within an arrow's flight of its top, when, looking back along the way they had come, they saw a lake spreading below them where once the city had been. Every building was gone except their own little cottage, which stood alone in the spreading waters. For a moment their eyes filled as they contemplated the dreadful fate of their neighbors. Then their eyes widened with amazement as they saw a change come over their dwelling. The wooden supports that had held up the thatched roof became marble columns. The thatch of the roof turned a brighter yellow, then shone resplendently as it changed to pure gold. The dirt floor became smooth marble, and their humble little cottage stood at last revealed as a temple, a temple of the gods.

Zeus spoke and his voice was almost gentle. "Fine old man, and good old woman worthy of such a husband, tell

us what your wishes are. Anything you ask will be granted you."

Baucis and Philemon drew a little apart from the gods and whispered together briefly. Suddenly they were nodding happily in agreement and, turning quickly, approached the gods again.

"It is our wish," said Philemon, "that we may be the priests of the new temple which stands now where our little house once stood. And since we have passed all our lives here in love and harmony, we ask that we may quit this life at the same moment. May I never live to see her grave, nor she mine."

Their prayer was granted.

For the rest of their lives they were keepers of the temple.

One day Baucis and Philemon, now very, very old, were standing outside the temple talking of the days when it was their humble, cozy cottage and of the happy life they had had together in it. All at once, Baucis saw Philemon putting forth leaves. At the same moment, Philemon saw Baucis changing. As they watched each other, leafy crowns formed around their heads. They had just time to say to each other, "Farewell, dear companion," when bark closed over their lips, silencing them forever. Swiftly the change continued until their bodies were covered with bark, and they stood rooted in the ground. Two trees growing from a single trunk, one an oak, the other a linden.

Europa

The sad story of Io proved how the love of Zeus could bring suffering to a mortal maiden. The story of another love of his, Europa, is happier.

One morning this lovely princess wakened from a strange dream: two women had been contesting for her. One seemed like a lady of her father's kingdom, but the other was a stranger, robed in a foreign costume. She held Europa with strong hands and spoke in a severe voice.

"It is the will of Zeus," she insisted, "that Europa shall be my prize."

The princess sprang from bed, glad that it was all a dream. Still, that strange woman held a fascination for her; she almost felt a longing in her heart, and impulsively she murmured a prayer.

"Ye blessed gods, let the stranger claim me. Let the dream come true."

With a light laugh at her own folly, Europa dressed hurriedly. Running from her bedchamber, she summoned her playmates, daughters of her father's court. The girls were lovely to look upon as they came gladly at their princess's call. But loveliest of all was Europa.

Gaily the maidens trooped out of the king's protecting courtyard and went straight to a wide and flowering meadow beside the sea. It was that time of the spring when the flowers were at their best. Each girl had a woven basket, intricately wrought and beautiful, swinging from her arm. But Europa's was most beautiful of all, for it had been made by Hephaestus, who had created the bewitching and foolish Pandora.

What a stretch of color and fragrance lay before them! Violets and yellow crocus, hyacinth and creeping thyme. Along the edges of the river, curving in wide loops through the flat meadow as it lazed its way to the sea, the hyacinth bent its head, nodding at its own reflection in the quiet water. The girls picked the blossoms and inhaled the sweetness of each handful before carefully laying it in their baskets. But it remained for Europa to find the most fragrant blooms of all. Standing amid the meadow flowers, she called to her companions and held above her head a crimson spray, a branch of the wild rose.

On this fair spring morning, Zeus, too, was enjoying the beauties of earth. He had rolled the mists away from Mount Olympus and sat contemplating the bright sunshine, the sea shimmering under the sun, and the silver glint of the rivers gliding to meet it. He noted the bright new green of oaks upon the hillsides and the flowered pattern that lay upon the meadows. Suddenly his gaze sharpened as he beheld a group of wonderfully attractive girls frolicking among the flowers in a meadow beside the sea. Just as Zeus's eye focused on Europa, Eros, god of love, let fly one of his bright arrows. Swiftly it pierced to the heart of the Father of Gods, and straightway he fell madly in love. He immediately began to think of some way of possessing that mortal maiden without arousing the suspicions of jealous Hera, who on this fateful day was, happily, absent from Olympus.

Above the meadow, on a gentle slope, a herd of cattle was grazing. Zeus summoned Hermes to him and bade him descend to Earth and drive the herd of cattle across the meadow toward the sea.

"Drive them to the very edge of the meadow, to where the salt grasses stand stiffly above the wet and shining sand," he told Hermes. The swift-footed messenger of the gods sped away quickly to carry out his orders.

Having filled their baskets, Europa and her maidens were seated on the ground, the bright flowers strewn among them as they plaited garlands to hang in honor of the gods. All at once they were aware of a herd of cattle moving quietly across the meadow toward the ocean. There was a bull with them, but such a bull as none of them had ever seen before. Its color was a gleaming chestnut, its horns were small and curved like jewels. In the very middle of its forehead there was a perfect crescent, as white and gleaming as the young moon. The bull was Zeus in disguise. As the girls' startled eyes filled with admiration of his beauty, he left the herd and slowly approached them. The girls got to their feet, afraid, but the bull moved so gently, halting before them with such a meek manner, that they lost all fear and crowded around him. They stroked his mighty shoulders and felt the smooth muscles beneath the satiny skin. Europa dared to put an arm around his neck, and the bull put out his tongue and licked her cheek. At this the girls all laughed. But Europa, undaunted, wiped the bull's black muzzle and returned the caress. Next she hung a garland around his horns, and when she had adjusted it to suit her, the bull lay down at her feet, presenting his broad back as if inviting her to seat herself on it.

"Look," she cried to her companions. "He wants us to climb on his back. Come, dear playmates, here is real adventure. He can carry all of us. Do not be afraid, for see how gentle he is. He seems more man than bull and lacks only speech to prove it. Come let us ride."

So saying she leaped upon the bull's back. No sooner had she done so than he rose to his feet and began walking toward the shoreline. The other maidens ran to catch up with him, bidding him stop so that they too might ride, but the bull quickened his steps. In another moment he was running, and they were left behind.

Europa turned and held out her arms to her comrades and called piteously to them, but the bull increased his speed and she feared to jump to the ground. The bull came to where the sea waves were flinging themselves upon the hard sand, and he waded into them, hardly halting in his stride. Instantly, the waves quieted before him, and the sea spread out smoothly as he cut a path through it. Europa seized one of his horns in her right hand. With the other she gathered up her long purple robe. The sea wind caught it and swelled it out like a sail behind her.

Thus they traveled over the waters until the land was lost to sight, and Europa could see only the blue depths below her and the blue sky above. Suddenly out of those depths came the ocean creatures. Dolphins rose above the surface, plunging and leaping about the bull and the frightened maiden. The Nereids, nymphs of the sea, appeared riding on great fishes, their hands resting lightly on the finny backs, their long tresses streaming in the breeze of their passing. Poseidon himself appeared upon the waters to assist his brother in his passage through them. Triton came, blowing a sound as merry as a wedding tune on his conch shell.

Europa was by now fully aware that this was no ordinary bull on which she rode as on a ship. Nor would these sea creatures escort in this way the mere leader of a cattle herd. Some god's will was at work here, and with this conviction she spoke.

"Where are you taking me bull-god, and who are you that the sea parts at your feet and the creatures of ocean guide your way? Are you a god as I suspect?"

And the bull answered her, "Have courage, gentle

maiden, and do not be afraid of the spreading waters. Though I wear the form of a bull, I am Zeus, father of gods and of men. Soon we shall arrive at Crete, the place of my birth. There you shall become my wife and the mother of strong sons."

They reached the shores of Crete and the great beast heaved himself out of the water. Europa slipped from his wide back. But when she turned again to face him, the bull had vanished, and in his place stood the god. He took Europa's hand and declared his love for her. And she let her hand rest in his and promised to love him in return.

In time, three sons were born to Europa. One of these was Minos, whose story you shall hear. As for that princess, her fame has never died. A continent bears her name, the continent we know as Europe.

The Story
of Cadmus

When Europa's maidens saw the great bull plunge into
the sea and swim away with their princess, they ran sorrowing to the palace to report what had happened to
King Agenor, her father. The king was outraged and
deeply grieved at what he heard, for he loved his daughter. He quickly summoned her three brothers before
him and bade them start out at once and seek the world
over until they found their sister, and not to return
home without her.

The three brothers set forth, each attended by a group
of servants. They traveled in different directions, for they
did not know in what part of the world to seek Europa.
After wandering across plains and over mountains and
through several provinces, two of the brothers abandoned the search, and, not daring to return home with-

out their sister, settled in foreign lands to spend the remainder of their lives.

But the third brother, Cadmus, as weary of the search as they, decided to seek advice at a cave that was famous for its oracle. This was the Castalian cave, which got its name in the following way.

One day the god Apollo, struck by the beauty of a nymph called Castalia, pursued her into a mountain fastness. The shy nymph, frightened by the god's wooing, threw herself into a deep spring that gushed from the mouth of a dark cave reaching back into the mountainside, and she drowned. Apollo, rushing up too late to save her and feeling remorse for what had happened, bestowed upon the cave the power of prophecy through an oracle that spoke out of it. And ever after it was known as the Castalian cave.

So now Cadmus sought this cave to ask its oracle what land he should settle in. All his weary wandering had failed to find Europa, and he feared the task was hopeless. Yet, like his brothers, he knew better than to return to King Agenor without her. The oracle answered his question saying, "When you leave this place, keep traveling until you come upon a heifer too young to have known the yoke. Follow to where she will lead you, and where she will at last lie down to rest, there you will build a city and you will call it Thebes."

Cadmus and his servants left the cave and had gone only a little distance from it when they beheld a heifer moving slowly in front of them. They followed obediently where she led, across a shallow stream and down the mountain and into a fertile plain. There the heifer stopped and lifted her head to heaven. She lowed gently, then folded her forefeet under her, and lay down. At this sign, Cadmus stooped and kissed the ground. Then raising his eyes to the surrounding hills, he considered their protecting heights and felt that here was a good spot to build his city. But first he wished to make a sacrifice to Zeus. In preparation for this he ordered his servants to go to the grove at the base of the nearest hill and here to procure the pure water so necessary to their offering.

The men started off willingly enough, glad that their long wandering was over. The grove they entered was an ancient one. It had never echoed to the sound of a woodman's ax. The trunks of the huge trees rose gnarled and twisted, while at their base, as if crowded out of the ground, hoary roots protruded in tangled clusters. Mighty branches met overhead through which the sun's rays filtered in an eerie twilight. No grass grew underfoot, but such an age-old carpeting of leaves had gathered there that the men moved soundlessly along the forest aisles in a silence as eerie as the light.

Suddenly in the stillness the men caught the sound of running water. Eagerly they hastened toward it and came upon a cave, surrounded by bushes, from which a stream of water flowed under a low arch.

The men dipped their jars into the bubbling spring. But no sooner had they done so, than there came gliding

forth from that cave a huge and hissing serpent. Its head
was a metallic blue and its awful slathering mouth, open
to free its three darting tongues, showed three rows of
poisonous fangs. Swiftly its scaly body oozed from under
that low arch, coil upon coil. The men dropped their
jars, and their cheeks whitened as they beheld the dreadful dragon so close upon them. They tried to run, but
fear and horror had numbed them so that they stood
helpless as birds before a garden snake. Mercilessly the
serpent fell upon them. Some he slew with his poisonous
fangs. Others he crushed in the coils of his powerful
body. Soon all the servants of Cadmus lay dead beside
the spring, the dragon coiled among them, his body
glistening darkly in the ghostly light.

Now Cadmus, waiting in the plain, wondered why it
was taking his men so long to find water. Surely that
towering grove at the base of the hill had had its roots
plentifully watered during the time it had grown there.
There must be a spring in such a place, with a stream
flowing from it. At last, when the sun stood midway in
the heavens, marking the middle of the day, Cadmus determined to go in search of his men. He wrapped a lion's
skin about his body as a kind of shield, then he took up
both his javelin and his spear. His best weapon, however, was his courageous heart. He set out from the plain
and approached the grove. He had entered but a little
way when he came upon the lifeless bodies of his servants
and the dragon coiled among them, its bloodied mouth
making all too plain how they had died.

Cadmus cried out with rage and grief. "Oh, my faithful comrades, I will take revenge upon this monster in return for your poor lives, or I will join you in death." Saying this, Cadmus seized a huge stone and hurled it at the serpent. Its force would have breached a fortress wall. But though it angered the monster, it bounced harmlessly from its coils. The dragon lifted its head above its coiled body and a fearful hissing filled the grove. Cadmus threw his javelin at the pale underside of the huge snake, and this time the javelin pierced the monster's hide. It lowered its head to bite at the javelin which was causing it intense pain. Struggling to withdraw the weapon, the serpent bit off the shaft of the iron head which continued to pierce it. Wild with rage and pain and pouring venom from its nostrils, it dropped its head and began gliding toward Cadmus, its great body like a tree trunk sliding along the ground. As it came toward him, Cadmus drew back step by step, always holding his spear before the monster's open jaws. The serpent darted its head at the weapon, seeking to bite off its iron point, but always Cadmus managed to keep it just beyond its reach. At last the hero saw his chance. The dragon had raised itself again and was starting to coil in order to thrust itself like a spring. Its head came back against a tree, and on that instant Cadmus threw the spear. It pierced the monster's neck clear through and stuck into the tree, nailing the dragon to it. Panting, Cadmus stood and watched the frightful death struggle. The tree bent with the serpent's thrashings, but it could not withdraw the

spear from the tree trunk. Gradually its efforts weakened, and at last it hung dead.

While Cadmus stood marveling at the great size and hideousness of the slain monster, he heard a voice speaking to him there in the deep wood. He looked around quickly, but could see no one. And so he knew a god was speaking.

"Take the dragon's teeth and sow them in the ground."

Cadmus did not hesitate to obey the strange command. With powerful fingers he wrenched the dragon's teeth from its jaws and carried them to the plain. There he dug a shallow furrow in the soil and scattered the teeth in it like a farmer sowing seed. Next he covered the furrow with dirt. Hardly had he done this than the soil began to stir. Sharp glistening points of metal appeared and, rapidly growing out of the earth, revealed themselves as points of spears. Next helmeted heads followed the spears out of the furrow, then shoulders and bodies of armored soldiers. Cadmus was frightened when he saw this host of armed men standing where the furrow had been, for he was certain they meant to attack him. But one of them spoke, setting his mind at rest.

"This is a war between brothers. Do not meddle with what does not concern you."

With that, the warrior swung about and began attacking the one next to him. Others began fighting all along the line, and their swords rang on their shields, in the fierce combat that began. Brother against brother they fought until all but five were dead. One of these suddenly threw his sword to the ground saying, "Enough of this slaughter. Let us make peace among us." The others were all too willing to heed his words. They, too, flung down their weapons, and the war was over.

The five offered to join their fortunes with Cadmus. He welcomed their comradeship, and, with their help, Cadmus built the city of Thebes as the oracle at the Castalian cave had directed him to do.

In time Zeus bestowed a bride upon Cadmus. She was Harmonia, a daughter of the gods and hence immortal. So important was this marriage to the inhabitants of Olympus that they descended to earth to celebrate it in Cadmus's city of Thebes. Zeus himself presided over the wedding feast and Hephaestus presented the bride with a wondrous necklace of his own making.

But for all the honor and happiness which marked the marriage of Cadmus and Harmonia, a curse seemed to hover over the House of Thebes. Several sons and daughters were born to them and all met terrible fates. It seemed as if the curse stemmed from the killing of the dragon which had been a special pride of Ares, god of war.

One day Cadmus said to Harmonia, "If a serpent is so precious to the gods, then would that I, too, might become a serpent."

No sooner had he spoken these fateful words than his manly body began to change. Before his wife's horrified eyes, Cadmus became a serpent, though a rather small and harmless one. She prayed at once to be allowed to share his fate, and her prayer was granted. Together they glided off into a quiet wood, where you may come upon them any day stretched along the bank of a stream or coiled sunning on a smooth flat stone.

The Story
of Theseus

THE BULL-MAN

One of the sons of Europa was Minos, who eventually
became king of Crete, the island to which Zeus in the
form of a bull had taken Europa.

As soon as he had been named to the throne, Minos
went to the seashore to offer sacrifice to Zeus, for he was
mindful of the gods. It was a day suited to a celebration.
The sun shone brightly, while sea birds dipped and
glided above the sparkling blue waters edged by golden
sands.

Minos strode into the first line of gently breaking
waves and, lifting his arms above his head, addressed
the god of the sea, Poseidon.

"Earth-shaker, giver of horses, who commands the
winds and the surging sea, hear me now. I wish to offer 61

a sacrifice to your brother, Zeus, hurler of thunderbolts. Send me then a victim worthy of the Father of Gods."

A large crowd of people had followed their new king to the shore and now stood closely packed on the sand behind him. But not a sound was heard from all that multitude as every eye fastened on the waters and men held their breath and waited the effect of King Minos's words.

All at once, out where the ocean swells rose smooth and oily, there was a stir of water. Then a head appeared above the surface, a bull's head with short curving horns. Great shoulders, white as sea foam, thrust themselves above the water and a bull began swimming strongly toward the shore. A murmur arose from the crowd, and Minos lowered his arms, backing a little as the bull advanced toward him. At last the king and the sea bull faced each other, and in the king's heart greed began to form. This animal was too beautiful and fine to be killed, even as a sacrifice to Zeus. What an addition he would be to the king's own herd! He would sire calves that would be the envy of everyone who saw them.

So Minos ordered that the bull be led away and safely confined. The best animal from the king's herd was brought as a substitute and offered up as the sacrifice.

Now Poseidon was fully aware of all that had happened, and he was filled with fury. An angry god is a vengeful god, and Poseidon punished Minos, who had cheated Zeus. He made the bull mad. It raged about the countryside, destroying crops and threatening the life of anyone in its way. But worse was to follow before the sea bull could be removed from Crete. The first calf sired by this bull was a terrible monster, half bull and half man. Thus did Poseidon avenge the dishonoring of his brother Zeus.

When news reached Minos of the birth of this half-human creature, his first instinct was to kill it. But a second thought forbade this. The bull which had sired this monster was a gift of the gods; it would be highly dangerous to destroy its offspring. So Minos let the monster live. But then a new problem presented itself. It was soon discovered that the Minotaur, as the monster was called, would eat nothing but human flesh. Minos promptly ordered it to be held behind strong barricades. But nothing seemed strong enough to hold the Minotaur.

Then Minos called to him a clever fellow named Daedalus. He was a great inventor and a sculptor who had created statues that moved. For some time Daedalus had been living at the palace of King Minos, who was happy to use the inventor's skills in any way he could. As a result, his palace was famed throughout the ancient world.

"My clever friend," began the king when Daedalus appeared before him. "I am much troubled by a monster which has appeared among my herds. It is the product of the bull which Poseidon sent me out of the sea, and which, in my mercy, I decided not to sacrifice, substituting my best herd bull in its place. But now it appears that in acting as I did I angered the god, for he has stricken the bull with madness and made this first calf of his a monster, half bull and half man."

Daedalus smiled. "I am well aware of this, Minos. And more. The Minotaur eats human flesh and you want him shut away from the world."

Minos nodded.

"I have a plan," said Daedalus.

"Let me hear it," said the king.

Daedalus outlined his scheme quickly,. for he had already given it much thought. His plan was to build beneath the palace a labyrinth of such numerous and puzzling mazes that no one who wandered into it could ever find his way out again. In the very heart of this tangle of dead ends, they would place the Minotaur. And though he might wander out from this central place, not even the Minotaur could find his way out of the maze.

"And when he hungers," said Daedalus, "you can turn a slave into the labyrinth for him to find."

So the Labyrinth was begun. Hundreds of slaves were set to digging in the light of hundreds of torches in the ground under the palace. No slave knew the plan of what he dug, and no slave was allowed to work two days in the same spot. The mazes reached deep into the bowels of the earth, their sides reaching up like the slopes of a hill. In the very center was a round, level space, the resting place of the Minotaur. When all was ready, the monster was driven into it, and there he remained.

As Daedalus had suggested, every now and then a slave was thrown into the Labyrinth to appease the monster's hunger. It was a dreadful fate. In the dim and shadowy passages, the luckless victim never knew when he would come upon the Minotaur; or, wandering helplessly, when he might follow a passage to the heart of the maze to find the creature awaiting him.

News of the Labyrinth and its victims soon spread beyond the palace and the people murmured angrily that even a disobedient slave should not be treated so.

Then war came to Crete, a war which Minos won. Youths and maidens in the form of tribute from his former enemies came to take the place of slaves in the Labyrinth. It happened in this way.

Minos had a son, Androgeos, whom he loved. When this lad had grown, he expressed a wish to travel away from the island of Crete to other lands and kingdoms. This his father gladly allowed, and the young prince set forth with a group of his companions. All went well until he came to Athens. There the king, Aegeus, sent him on a dangerous mission. A great white bull had been ravaging the countryside near Marathon, and Aegeus suggested that Androgeos could test his courage and his skill at arms by ridding the country of this bull. The creature was none other than the bull Poseidon had sent out of the sea to Minos as a sacrifice to Zeus and which he had later made mad. It was the very same bull which had sired the Minotaur.

Aegeus, who was not an unkind man, may not have known of the mad bull's origins or of his special fierceness. But in any case, he was behaving badly as a host, for he was sending a guest into certain danger, and this the gods could hardly forgive. Yet, it was poor, brave Androgeos who paid with his life for Aegeus's lapse, for the bull killed him. In grief and anger, Minos declared war upon Aegeus to avenge his son's death.

As might be expected, the war went badly for Athens. Minos was powerful, with many allies. To make sure of Aegeus's defeat, the gods sent a plague upon Athens, which so weakened that city that she could not withstand Minos's armies. Athens fell and Minos claimed from it a dreadful tribute. Every nine years the city was to send to Crete seven maids and seven lads, who would be thrown into the Labyrinth to starve or be devoured by the Minotaur.

These young people were chosen by lot from among the highest born citizens of Athens. Twenty-eight of Athens's finest had gone to feed the Minotaur before the city was at last delivered from its cruel fate by a great hero. His name was Theseus.

THE BIRTH OF THESEUS

A year or two after his war with Crete, King Aegeus went on a visit to Troezen, a province south of Athens ruled over by King Pittheus. Aegeus was growing old and had no children, while the fifty sons of his brother Pallas lounged around his city of Athens, mocking his childlessness and threatening to take over his kingdom. Aegeus wished to discuss this problem with his friend, King Pittheus.

Now it happened that this king had a beautiful daughter named Aethra. Many noble lads from all over Greece had come to Troezen seeking her hand in marriage, but Pittheus had refused them all. He had received an oracle that his daughter would marry a great king, and though this marriage would bring Aethra no honor in itself, it would result in a son who would be famous throughout all the world and through all the ages to come. Pittheus welcomed the idea of such a grandson.

Aegeus's visit had hardly begun when he met Pittheus's lovely daughter and immediately fell in love with her. But now a fresh problem presented itself. Aegeus already had a wife, aging like himself. Despite his years, Aegeus longed for an heir and he longed for Aethra. At last he spoke to Pittheus of his great desire.

"Let me marry your daughter," he pleaded, "and if a son is born of our union, he will inherit my kingdom after my death."

"But you have a wife," objected Pittheus.

"True," admitted Aegeus. "My marriage with Aethra will have to remain secret."

"How can a son born of a secret marriage establish his right to your throne?" asked Pittheus.

"I shall arrange for that," promised Aegeus.

It was not unusual in those times for a king to have two wives, and Pittheus, mindful of the oracle he had received, decided to let Aegeus marry Aethra secretly. So the wedding was performed, the bride, as was the custom in those days, having nothing whatever to say about it.

When at last it was necessary for Aegeus to return to Athens, he said to his bride, "Come with me; I have a secret to share with you."

He led the girl away from her father's palace and into the heart of a deep wood. Here was a pool, and at one side of it lay a huge and mossy stone. Aegeus bent down and, seizing one edge of the stone in both hands, succeeded in lifting it from the ground. Under it was concealed a sword and a pair of sandals.

"If the gods are kind and our marriage is blessed with a son, I want you to bring him here when he is approaching manhood and bid him raise this stone. If he is able to lift it as I have, then let him put on the sandals and take up the sword and come to me in Athens."

So saying, he took leave of Aethra and returned to his own kingdom.

The gods were kind, and a little while after her husband's departure, Aethra gave birth to a boy. He was a wondrous babe, lusty and strong and perfect in face and figure. They named him Theseus. Pittheus smiled often as he watched this grandson grow from infancy to child-hood. Surely this was the lad the oracle had promised. Soon young Theseus gave proof of this.

On a day after he had reached his seventh year, a huge man strode into the courtyard of Pittheus's palace where Theseus and his companions were at play. The giant wore a lion's skin and carried an immense club balanced on one of his broad shoulders. At the sight of this fearsome creature, all the boys ran for cover—all but Theseus, who stood his ground and watched the giant's approach. The powerful man, who was none other than the famed Heracles, let out a great roar of laughter at the sight of one small boy blocking his path. But Theseus was not accustomed to being mocked. The laughter angered him, and he threw himself at Heracles, butting his head hard against the giant's knees. The laughter rang out louder as Heracles reached down a hand and lifted the boy high into the air as easily as he might have wafted a feather aloft.

"And who is this young fellow who would take issue with Heracles?" he demanded in a voice that filled the courtyard.

Theseus's eyes widened as he dangled uncomfortably from the great hand. Heracles! Every boy knew of Heracles, the greatest hero of the ancient world.

The giant lowered Theseus to the ground and grinned down at him. "I like your courage, lad. Let me know your name, for someday, I doubt not, it will be as famous as my own."

"I am Theseus, grandson of Pittheus."

"Then let us be friends, brave Theseus, and proud to call each other friend."

From that day the young Theseus took Heracles as his model.

THESEUS GOES TO ATHENS

When Theseus was sixteen years old, his mother decided the time had come to test him. The promise of his child-hood was now fulfilled in this tall, strong lad who walked beside her as she led him to the grove where the heavy stone lay. He seemed older than his sixteen years. A man's gravity rested in his eyes, and his lips, curving with the gentleness of youth, were firm above a chin already covered with golden down. Aëthra could be proud of her son as they approached the mossy stone. They stopped and Theseus smiled down tenderly at his mother, whose sudden desire to bring him here seemed a mere, puzzling, whim.

She looked up at him, her face serious. "I have brought you here as your father directed me long ago," she said. "And now my heart is all confused. If you are strong enough to lift that stone, then you will go from me. If you fail to lift it, then you will stay beside me for another year. That would be sweet, and yet, my son, I think I want you to be strong."

Without replying to her, Theseus bent and laid his hands against the stone. He moved them until he found the grip he wanted. Suddenly his shoulders bunched, and the muscles of his thighs bulged below his short tunic. Aethra watched as slowly, slowly the stone broke free of the earth which bound it. With a sudden lurch and heave, Theseus rolled it to one side. The sword and sandals lay revealed.

Aethra waited until the lad's heaving chest had somewhat quieted, and then she said, "Your father placed those things there. When you were old enough and strong enough to find them, you were to take them up and travel to Athens where he is king. When he sees these sandals and this sword, he will recognize you as his son."

Theseus took up the sword and the sandals, and they returned to the palace where Pittheus awaited them.

"So you are a man now," declared the king, smiling upon his grandson and daughter as they stood before him.

"My mother tells me that I am to go in search of my father as he directed," said Theseus proudly.

"That you shall, and this very day I shall order a ship to be made ready to take you to Athens," said Pittheus.

"I thank you for your kindness," said Theseus, "but I intend to go by land."

Aethra gasped and put out a hand. "No, no, my son," she cried. "Surely you have heard of the terrible dangers that lie along the land route between Troezen and Athens. It is death to travel that road."

"Nonetheless, I shall take it. Would Heracles avoid its dangers? I think not. Nor shall I."

Thus spoke Theseus in the pride of his young manhood. All the pleading of Pittheus and Aethra could not change his mind. So at last, wearing his father's sword and sandals, Theseus took leave of them and started on his perilous journey.

The narrow stretch of land he was about to travel separated two seas. It was the Isthmus of Corinth. Centuries later, a canal would be cut across this isthmus, uniting the waters. In Theseus's time, this route was rarely traveled, for fearful monsters lay in wait along it. Theseus of course knew of them all and was ready for them.

The first he came upon was a giant named Periphetes. He always carried an iron club with which he smashed the skulls of luckless travelers. When he caught sight of Theseus, he rushed upon the youth, club raised. But like so many Greek youths, Theseus was a skilled boxer and wrestler. He cleverly knocked the giant off balance, then twisted his arm behind his back so painfully that Periphetes dropped the club, which Theseus seized. In another instant the cruel monster lay dead at the lad's feet, his skull crushed by his own weapon. So Theseus dealt with the first of the dreadful dangers.

Theseus rested from his labors that night in Periphetes's own hut. At dawn next morning, he took up his sword and the iron club and started in search of his next adventure. Leaving the open meadows, he entered a pine forest. Before long he saw frightful evidence of danger. Dangling from the tops of pine trees were the remains of broken bodies. Theseus knew at once that he had come to the lair of Sinis, the Pine Bender. He was called this because whenever anyone came within his reach, he bent down the tops of two pine trees, bound his victim to them, then let the trees spring apart, tearing the prisoner in two. Now it was Theseus's turn to meet this cruel death. As Sinis rushed upon him, the young hero struck him with the iron club. Then bending two pine trees to the ground, Theseus bound Sinis to them with his own ropes and let the trees spring aloft. Thus the isthmus was rid of another evil.

On the following day, Theseus found his road narrowing to a rocky path that ran along the side of a cliff high above the sea. He knew that now he was close to the abode of Sciron, who demanded to have his feet washed by any traveler who appeared. While the frightened stranger was obeying the command, Sciron would lift a foot and kick his victim off the cliff to the rocks below, where a huge turtle would devour him.

Rounding a bend in the path, Theseus now came upon a huge, rough-looking man sitting squarely in the middle of it. This was Sciron.

"Ho, stranger," cried the man. "Come here and serve your betters. I would have you wash my feet."

Theseus knelt down, acting as if he suspected nothing. But when he had the brute's confidence, the lad grabbed him by a foot and flung him over the cliff's edge.

"This time you shall feed your turtle yourself," he called down. "And it's the last such dining he will ever do."

Now Theseus was coming near the city of Eleusis, where he was to meet with another savage. This man was Cercyon, a wrestler who in his time had killed many men. Catching sight of Theseus, he bellowed a challenge to him. In an instant, the two were struggling in a death match. Theseus needed all his great skill as a wrestler, for Cercyon was bigger and stronger and more experienced than he. But Theseus was the cleverer of the two and managed at last to get a stranglehold on his enemy, slowly forcing the life out of him.

He continued on his way, his heart rejoicing that only one more perilous trial lay between him and the city of Athens. In a high tower overlooking the road lived a robber who was called Procrustes, the Stretcher. Procrustes would come forth from his tower and warmly welcome any stranger unlucky enough to journey this way. He would take the stranger into his tower, feed him well, then, when it was time for sleep, would show him to his bed. But the bed of Procrustes was no ordinary bed. It fit whoever laid himself upon it; Procrustes saw to that. For if the stranger was too short for the bed, the robber stretched him out until his bones parted from one another. If the bed was too short, the stranger's head was lopped off. Now it was Theseus's turn to receive Procrustes's cruel hospitality.

He entered the tower giving no sign that he knew

what Procrustes intended. But when dinner was over and Procrustes led his guest to the bed, Theseus seized the robber and hurled him onto it. He cut off his head with the sword of Aegeus, and so it was that Procrustes was made to fit his own bed. The world was rid of another evil. Without further adventure, Theseus came to Athens.

Much to his surprise, news of his heroic deeds had traveled faster than he. As soon as it was known that Theseus had entered the city, the people poured into the streets to give him a hero's welcome and to escort him to the king's palace.

Not long before this time, a certain sorceress had come to live with King Aegeus. Her name was Medea, and her heart was evil. By means of her witch's wiles, she knew all about Theseus, and she feared that he would cause her to be banished from Athens. She had managed to persuade Aegeus, now a lonely, wifeless old man, to make her his wife, and she did not intend that this young son of his should come to power. So she made plans to be rid of him. King Aegeus fell in with her plans. She easily convinced him that this young hero was a threat to his throne, while concealing from the old man the fact that Theseus was his son.

Hearing the noise outside the palace, she drew the old king to a window that overlooked the street down which a mob of people was approaching, Theseus leading them.

"Do you see that?" cried Medea. "The people have

found a hero. In another day they will have found a new king. We must get rid of this upstart before he can get rid of you."

Aegeus eyed the wildly cheering throng and sudden fear pinched his heart. He knew his people were weary of his senile ways, nor did they trust his attachment to this witch under whose spell he had fallen. He feared the people might indeed place such a young and attractive hero on his throne. Aegeus did not recognize his son, for Theseus carried the sandals in a bag slung over his shoulder, and the sword was hidden in its scabbard.

"Leave it all to me," whispered Medea into the old man's ear. "Welcome him as befits a hero, and trust the rest to me."

Aegeus nodded his head slowly.

Theseus, as he approached the palace, felt increasing excitement. He was about to greet his father!

Aegeus was sitting in his throne room when Theseus was brought into the palace by the chief nobles of the city. While Theseus stood quietly gazing upon this old man who was his father, he heard one of the nobles telling the king of the dangers he had come through and about how he had rid the Isthmus of Corinth of its monsters.

The old king listened attentively, then cleared his throat and spoke.

"These are great deeds for one so young," he said, looking contemptuously upon Theseus. "Not even Heracles could make greater claims than you, yet you offer no proof of your bravery. I will believe you have done what you claim when you have killed the bull from Crete that has ravaged the land around Marathon and that killed the son of King Minos, thus causing us to send seven youths and seven maidens as tribute to Crete every ninth year."

It was Medea who had advised King Aegeus to make this demand upon Theseus, for she was sure the bull would kill the youth even as he had killed every other man who tried to fight him. She even thought that Theseus might refuse the challenge, thus forfeiting his hero's role and with it any chance of gaining the throne.

Angered by the king's expressed doubt of him, Theseus withstood the temptation to reveal himself. He would show his father what kind of man he had sired. Looking boldly upon the king, Theseus said quietly, "It shall be as the king desires. Tonight we will sacrifice the flesh of that bull to the god Apollo." He bowed courteously, then turned on his heel and left the throne room.

Alone, Theseus went at once to Marathon. There he met the bull and, seizing him by the horns, wrestled him to the ground and broke his neck. Then he dragged the carcass back to Athens where he sacrificed it that night at Apollo's temple on a hill high above the city.

Medea was furious when the news reached her. She decided that the only way to destroy Theseus was to poison him. There was to be a feast for the hero at the palace this very evening. She would mix a potion to put into his wine cup. So great was her evil influence over Aegeus that he agreed to this, since the hero threatened his throne even more after his latest deed.

Theseus, too, had made plans for this evening. He had decided that he would reveal himself during the feast. For this purpose, he put on the sandals and hung the sword in its scabbard over his shoulder as was the custom.

Before the king entered the feasting hall, Theseus was led to the place of honor next to the throne. Soon Aegeus appeared, Medea at his side. The king took his seat, but Medea remained standing, a golden goblet in her hand. Raising the goblet high, she proclaimed, "The first of the wine for the hero," and placed the cup before Theseus.

Meanwhile servants had brought in plates of meat and set them before each guest. Drawing his sword, Theseus cut the meat on his plate, then, rising, he took up the goblet to toast the king.

But Aegeus had seen the sword and recognized it. This was his son! Leaping to his feet, he dashed the cup from Theseus's hand just before it touched his lips. The goblet fell with a crash, and the poison poured forth upon the stone floor. Medea fled from the hall. She later disappeared into the night in a winged chariot drawn by dragons and was seen no more in Athens.

Aegeus and Theseus faced one another. For a moment the old eyes looked beseechingly into the younger, then the king put out his arms, and Theseus with a glad cry flung himself upon his father's shoulder.

THESEUS MEETS THE MINOTAUR

Now Athens had a prince, and the old king's heart was glad. Glad, too, were the people. Only the fifty sons of Pallas, brother of the king, were angered by the sudden turn of events. Because they boasted openly that the new prince would never succeed to the throne while they lived, Theseus was determined that none of them would live much longer. Biding his time, and planning his strategy with care and cleverness, Theseus enlisted the help of certain young nobles who had declared undying allegiance to their hero and prince. Then, when Theseus deemed the time was right, he and his friends did battle with these traitorous nephews of his father and killed every one of them. So the succession was secured, and the last fear of King Aegeus was laid to rest.

But shortly there arose a more dreadful threat to his peace of mind.

Nine years had elapsed since the last seven youths and seven maids had sailed away from their dear city to find death as the victims of the Minotaur in the Labyrinth. The time had come for the third offer of tribute to King Minos of Crete. Loud was the sorrowing of parents as they faced the possibility of having their children torn from them to die a hideous death. The king and his nobles gathered together where the lots to choose the victims were to be drawn. The voices of the noble families rose against the king, who was responsible for this threat to their sons and daughters.

When Theseus heard the cries against his father, a brave plan formed in his mind. Hesitating only a moment, he sprang to his feet and faced the assembly.

"Choose only six youths," he cried. "I offer myself as the seventh. It is not fair that the king's son be spared. I will go to Crete with your sons and daughters, and there I shall subdue the Minotaur or die in the attempt."

It was in vain that Aegeus pleaded with Theseus to withdraw his offer. In vain he tried to persuade his son that the country would need his leadership, that it was folly to sacrifice himself, so favored by the gods, when any other youth would do as well.

"Dear Father," Theseus replied, "early in my life I took Heracles for my model. No more than Heracles will I turn away from danger. And the gods do favor me; I have proved that. Therefore it is my duty to face the Minotaur and perhaps put an end to this cruel tribute."

So they took ship, Theseus and his thirteen companions. Because of the sad nature of their journey, the ship was fitted with a black sail. But Aegeus had ordered a white sail to be put aboard. Then he made Theseus promise that if his mission were successful, he would sail into the port of Athens with the white sail in place. Thus would the king know that his son lived, and all the citizens of Athens would learn on sight that the tribute was ended.

Theseus promised, and the ship started out, its black sail a somber shadow upon the bright waters.

The crossing to Crete was uneventful. But as the black-sailed ship approached the stone jetty where its prisoners would be unloaded, Theseus saw a crowd. Beyond it, though a considerable distance from the shore, the palace of King Minos rose impressively, terrace upon terrace. The victims were soon marching toward it. As they came slowly up the long slope of the processional way, Theseus was awed by the vastness of the palace. Arriving at the top, the Athenians were led across a wide, open area and into a huge court enclosed with massive wooden columns, brilliantly colored. They crossed it to enter a narrow corridor and then were in a large room from which a wide stairway rose to the floor above. The walls were alive with paintings so vivid and real their figures seemed to move. Theseus was dazzled by the splendor. He vowed that if the gods should spare his life, he would build palaces and temples the equal of this in Athens when he became king.

As the young people started up the stairway to the hall where King Minos awaited them, Theseus saw that there were openings in the walls above the stairs through which the ladies of the court looked down upon the captives. One face in that crowd made him stop. He marveled that a mere human could possess such beauty. Was this then a goddess? Under his ardent gaze the face blushed, thus proclaiming it to be human, a girl quite as struck by Theseus's beauty as he was by hers. Neither gestured toward the other, yet something definite and final as an avowal passed between them. Thus did the daughter of King Minos, Ariadne, and the hero Theseus silently declare their instant love.

Ariadne was among those who thronged the throne room where the young captives were brought and presented to the king. She thought of the awful fate that awaited them, and she knew she would have to try to save Theseus and his companions, even though this betrayal of her father might cost her life.

That evening, Ariadne sought the inventor Daedalus where he strolled alone upon one of the high roof terraces of the palace. The princess was accompanied by a trusted serving woman.

Daedalus watched admiringly as Ariadne approached him across the paving under a sky full of stars.

"I have come, Daedalus, seeking your advice," she said. "It concerns the hero, Theseus. I want to save him."

Daedalus smiled. "I saw your gaze upon him today in the great hall and your visit is not altogether unexpected."

Ariadne was grateful that the starlight was not bright enough to betray the blush his words called into her cheeks.

"How can he be saved?" she whispered.

"He has come here vowing to kill the Minotaur. Only the gods can aid him in that combat."

"He has achieved many great feats," said Ariadne. "I believe that he will kill the Minotaur. But suppose he does? How will he then escape the Labyrinth? This is what I need to know, Daedalus."

"And when you have learned the secret, then what?" asked the inventor.

"I will take the word to him somehow," Ariadne replied.

Daedalus studied her gentle face for a moment in the light of the stars. "You are a brave girl," he said at last, "and I will help you."

She stepped closer to him. "Tell me quickly," she breathed.

"I have an idea," began Daedalus. "Like many good ideas, it is quite simple. One has only to think of it." His tone was slightly mocking as he thought of the several palace nobles who took a dim view of his accomplishments. They held that anyone might have done the same. One only had to have the idea first! "You must give Theseus a large spool of thread—silk would be best. Let him fasten the end of it to the doorpost at the entrance to the Labyrinth, unwinding it as he proceeds into those regions. When he has met with the Minotaur, and if he manages to kill him, he can wind up the string again, following it as he winds, until it brings him back to the entrance. Let his companions remain huddled there when he first goes in, and, when he comes again to the door, you must be the one to open it for him. Then be prepared to flee with Theseus and the others. Speed to his boat. But before setting sail, make sure he has scuttled the king's boats that lie in the harbor. That way, you will escape pursuit. For never doubt that Minos will want his blood—and yours."

Ariadne shuddered slightly and drew her scarf closer around her shoulders. "The risks are very great, I know. Yet I love him enough to risk anything for his sake." She looked up earnestly at the inventor. "Thank you, Daedalus. And if I never see you again, may the gods smile upon you and keep you safe."

With that she turned and quickly crossed the terrace. The serving woman stepped out of the shadows where she had been waiting and, walking just a step behind the princess, disappeared with her into the palace.

Later that same evening, the single guardsman posted outside the cell of the young Athenians was surprised to see a woman approaching along the dark corridor. Her head and features were hidden in a ragged scarf, and the rest of her attire was equally worn and poor. Obviously a beggar woman of the streets, thought the soldier, who had never beheld the face of his princess, Ariadne.

"I have come from the harbor," she said, "with a message for your prisoner Theseus. It is a last greeting from the pilot of the ship that brought him here."

"I have no orders to let anyone speak with Theseus," said the guard.

"The pilot told me to give you this." The girl held out a handful of coins.

The man, poor as he was ignorant, struggled with his conscience as he eyed the coins. This girl plainly was from the docks, a piece of harmless riffraff. And Theseus with all his comrades would soon be safely locked inside the Labyrinth with the fearsome Minotaur, where no one could be in contact with him again. Arriving at this thought, the guard hesitated no longer, but grinning cruelly, reached for the coins.

"Make it quick," he ordered as he shot the bolt to the cell door and rudely shoved the beggar girl inside.

The Athenians had leaped to their feet at the sound of the bolt. They were surprised to discover a girl where they had expected the armed guard that would escort them to the Labyrinth.

"I wish to speak with Theseus," whispered Ariadne into the darkness.

"Here is Theseus," said a voice close beside her.

She turned and clutched his tunic. "I am the Princess Ariadne," she said, her words spoken swiftly. "We have only an instant, so listen carefully."

Clearly and quickly she explained what Daedalus had told her, then, reaching into her ragged garment, she drew forth a spool of silk. "Here," she said, fumbling for his hand in the dark. "Hide it well and may the gods be with you."

Theseus had just taken the spool into his hand when again there came the sound of the drawn bolt. The door swung open, and a shaft of light fell aslant the cell. In that light, a wisp in rags, as silent and secret as a wraith, slipped through the door and along the corridor and out of sight.

Some time later, those within the cell heard the measured thud of marching feet and the clang of weapons. The guard had arrived to escort them to the Labyrinth.

Flanked by the soldiery, the fourteen Athenian youths and maidens trudged along dim corridors to dark and narrow staircases, which led them always down, down to the bottommost recesses of this vast palace. At last the captain of the guard called a halt. In the dim light of a single torch, Theseus, who stood at the head of the captive group, beheld a heavy door which seemed to close the side of a hill. They had reached the entrance to the Labyrinth!

The captain unbolted the door and pulled it slowly forward into the corridor. It came grudgingly, for it was heavy, and with it came a dreadful smell of sour earth and dampness. But overriding this, and striking a chill into every heart beating there, came the stink of beast and blood.

The captain motioned, and Theseus led the Athenians into the dark unknown. The door creaked shut behind them. Theseus put an ear tight against it and heard the bolt shoot home and the measured sound of retreating footsteps. Had a guard been left behind? Had Ariadne succeeded in hiding herself nearby? Would her frail strength be equal to the heavy bolt and door? These questions whirled through his mind as he tried to look about him, his eyes gradually becoming accustomed to the darkness.

In the long years since the Labyrinth had been constructed, Crete had suffered many earthquakes, which had opened slight cracks between the palace structure and this subterranean earthwork. What had once been totally dark now offered in places a grim, gray twilight, the difference between black and charcoal. During the day, a rare trace of sunlight filtered through a narrow crack. At night, as now, the faint glimmer from the torches lighting the palace's approaches here and there feebly pierced the gloom. Staring, Theseus could barely discern just such a dubious lightening of the darkness down the corridor.

He tied the thread to the doorpost while the others crowded around him.

"Feel this thread," he commanded them, "and remember where I have tied it. Let no one touch it, for if it breaks, I will never return to you, whether or not I conquer the Minotaur."

They stepped back from him obediently, but their whispers reached him from out of the dark.

"Take us with you, Theseus!"

"You are great, Theseus, but fourteen are better than one, even though he is a hero!"

Theseus silenced them. "How could fourteen follow this frail thread? In the darkness and in the confusion of the struggle it would surely be broken. Then what would become of us? Better sudden death than slow starvation. Do as I have commanded you, pray to the gods for me, and all may yet be well."

And so he took leave of them and, holding to the thread, unwound it carefully as he advanced cautiously toward that lighter dark in the surrounding darkness.

He continued blindly and bravely on, stopping now and then to listen, ever mindful of his slender lifeline. Once his heart leaped as a sound reached him. He crouched in the darkness, waiting. Was this the Minotaur? There it was again. His breathing tightened. Should he set the spool down, hoping to find it when the fight was over—if he lived? For the third time the sound came, and now he could define it. It was nothing more than a bit of dirt rolling down the steep side of the passageway. But it gave him an idea, and when again he came to a slightly lightened area, he stopped to consider the sloping wall above him. Yes, he thought it might be managed. Hurriedly, he slipped off his sandals and tucked them inside his belted tunic. He would need the grip of bare toes here.

Twice he leaped at the wall, only to slide back. But on the third try his toes held, and, clinging flat, he worked a toehold, and another and another. Inch by breathless inch, he wriggled upward until he came to a narrow ledge. It was a precarious perch, but he would make use of it until some better strategy came to mind. For Theseus had decided to fall upon the monster if he should come this way. Surprise has won many a battle, and Theseus was counting on the unexpectedness of his attack to give him the split-second advantage over the Minotaur that could make the difference between death and victory. So now he waited, his muscles tense, his ears straining for the first warning of the monster's approach.

He had not long to wait. His first awareness of the brute's approach was a sudden unexplainable, but utterly certain, knowledge of immediate danger. Nothing had moved in the shadows below him; no sound had reached his ears. Yet he *knew* the moment was now, and his every sense sharpened to meet it.

All at once he heard a quick and gentle *slap, slap, slap,* like someone running barefoot. Out of the wall of blackness into the region of shadow the Minotaur trotted. Theseus had an instant's sight of a bull's head and horns and mighty shoulders slimming down into a man's waist and legs and feet before he hurled himself down on that broad back.

The Minotaur met the attack with a bellow that shook the passageway, echoing and re-echoing throughout the Labyrinth as if a dozen bulls were trumpeting their rage. If heard above ground, it must have sounded like the muffled rumblings that announce an earthquake's dreaded approach. The monster raised its bull's forelegs above its head in an effort to seize the enemy, but its cloven hooves were powerless to pluck this menace off his back.

That one bellow was the only one Theseus allowed him. Thrusting his hands into the beast's wide nostrils, the hero forced the heavy head back so that the neck was stretched to the breaking point. Then with all his strength, Theseus drove a powerful blow against the monster's throat. There was a crunch of broken bone,

a cough, and blood began pouring from the Minotaur's mouth. Now Theseus slid from the bull-man's back, and, stepping in front of him, got inside his aimlessly waving hooves to deliver a telling blow to his heart. The Minotaur staggered and slowly sank to his knees. Now Theseus rushed in recklessly, and with blow after mighty blow ended the torment. In the dim and shadowy passage the Minotaur lay dead.

The hero waited only a moment, then tugging the silken thread gently, he rolled the spool off the ledge and began his slow, cautious return, winding the thread as he went.

ESCAPE

No time was spent in celebration of Theseus's return to his comrades. Even as they gasped out their first joy at what his return meant to all of them, Theseus was giving the signal that would cause Ariadne to open the door. If she was there. Theseus pressed his ear against the door to hear the welcome sound of the bolt being slowly drawn. Theseus put his shoulder against the door and it swung wide to reveal the startled girl, alone in the corridor.

Quickly they sped away, Ariadne and Theseus running beside each other as she led them along the secret windings of the underground regions. At this hour before the dawn the torches had almost burned out. The guards were sleepy and careless. No one saw the jubilant refugees as they slipped out of the palace and sped toward the harbor. Working swiftly, they scuttled as many ships as they could reach, then made for their own. Their pilot was awake and watching, marveling at the Cretan boats sinking out of sight one by one.

"Quick," said Theseus. "Run up the sail while we take to the oars."

The pilot leaped to carry out his orders, and soon the sail was in place, but hanging limp. With Ariadne safely aboard, the Athenians bent to the oars, and the boat shot away from the stone jetty. Stroke after stroke, and still all seemed quiet on the island of Crete. Now a puff of wind moved the sail, and a breeze filled it.

"Where to, master?" called the pilot as he settled in the stern, the rudder in his hand.

"Naxos," answered Theseus, shipping his oars. King Minos if he gave pursuit, would hardly look for them there since it was off course for Athens.

The run to Naxos left the fugitives hungry and thirsty. Only Theseus and Ariadne, wrapped in their love, seemed indifferent to such small discomfort. They fed on their happiness and thirsted only for the time when they could be safe and alone together. Nor did the others complain, so glad were they to be safe and soon home. The island proved to be verdant and well stocked with game. Before long, the pilot had set snares. He soon

had the game he caught roasting over a fire kindled
from the charcoal brazier aboard the boat.

That night, well fed and lulled by the gentle slap of
waves against the shore, they slept. Exhausted and
drained by the anxiety they had suffered for so long, they
slept the sleep of old dogs in the sun or kittens cuddled
against their dam's safe side. Only Theseus moaned and
tossed, struggling with the god of sleep, who had sent a
dreadful dream to vex his slumbers.

Dionysus, god of the vine, appeared before him in
this dream. "Do not take Ariadne to Athens with you,"
warned the god. "She is fated to become my bride and
thus win immortality. I love her well, and she will be
honored above all mortal women, as she deserves to be."

"She is deserving of such honor, I agree," Theseus
replied in his dream, "but we have vowed our love for
each other, and I cannot give her up, even for a god."

"Yet you must," replied Dionysus. "No mortal can
deny the gods with safety. Thus far they have favored
you, Theseus. But if you deny me Ariadne, it will go
hard with you forevermore."

"You are one god among many," said Theseus, "and
Ariadne is one woman out of all the earth. And she is
mine."

At these defiant words, the god's bright face darkened
in anger, but he kept his voice reasonable as he answered,
"Then consider this. Ariadne is the daughter of King
Minos at whose command twenty-eight of the choicest
youths and maidens among Athens' citizenry have met

hideous deaths. Will their fathers and mothers welcome that king's daughter as their future queen? Rather will they tear her limb from limb. Is your love so selfish you would take her into danger? Think again, Theseus."

The god vanished while the young prince tossed and moaned and at last awoke. He glanced quickly to where Ariadne lay in the leafy bower he had prepared to protect her against the night mists. He could faintly see the outline of her slender figure in the light of the approaching dawn. Then a spasm of pain crossed his face.

Dreams, he well knew, were portents. And his had been very real. The god's voice still sounded in his ears, its warning clear. Once again he saw the angry faces in that assembly where he had declared himself, and fear for Ariadne suddenly smothered every other emotion in him. Dionysus was right, as the gods always were. Minos's daughter must not go to Athens. Now he loved her enough to leave her. And the god had promised to be kind.

Quickly, Theseus rose and wakened his companions. They were aghast at what he proposed, yet they, too, saw at once that Ariadne could go to Athens only in peril of her life. Silently they stole aboard the boat while Theseus took a last farewell of his sleeping love. She lay with one arm crooked under her head, her cheek resting against the elbow. A small smile curved her sweet mouth and her lashes shadowed her cheek. Tears rushed into his eyes and such an ache into his throat that he groaned. She stirred. Theseus turned and sped toward the waiting boat. In sorrow and silence, they ran up the sail and drew away from the island of Naxos, where lay, all unsuspecting, the sleeping Ariadne.

Now each day since Theseus and his companions had sailed for Crete, old King Aegeus had taken his place on a high cliff commanding a far view of the waters. Day after day he sat there, offering prayers for the return of his son and the thirteen with him. Sometimes other sorrowing parents joined him. So he was not alone on this particular day when a sail was sighted approaching Athens. All saw it and dread seized their hearts. But still no one spoke, for the boat was yet too far distant to identify it. They watched its approach with anxious eyes.

Suddenly there came a cry, so full of despair and suffering that no one there could ever again quite rid his ears of it. The old king had risen from his seat. His knotted fists were raised above his head as if to pummel the sky. "My son, my son!" he shrieked. Then, taking a step toward the cliff's edge, he shook a gnarled fist at the black sail that came into his view, crying, "My life ends with yours."

Before anyone could stop him, Aegeus hurled himself over the cliff's edge, plunging a thousand feet into the sea below.

Theseus and his companions, numb with sorrow at the loss of Ariadne, had forgotten to substitute the white sail for the black one. Their grief for the abandoned princess had quite wiped out of their minds their promise to King Aegeus.

When at last they came into port and made their way into the city, they were unprepared for the sad faces they met along their way. When the news of this fresh loss was borne to him, Theseus felt as if his heart could not endure its pain. He ordered a funeral prepared such as befitted an honored king, then took over the reins of government himself.

Theseus was a wise ruler, consolidating his kingdom, fortifying the city, and subduing all enemies who moved against it. He kept the vow made in Crete, erecting temples and palaces so that Athens became famed for beauty as well as good government. Though he married several times, he was never happy in love again, and he died when his last wife betrayed him. But still he lives in memory as the true founder of Athens and one of the great heroes of all time.

Daedalus

Daedalus was a clever man. He was also a prudent one. On the evening that Ariadne visited him on the starlit terrace of the great palace of King Minos, he had already made plans to leave that island. They were secret plans, for well he knew that Minos would never willingly let his inventor go. Moreover, circumstances had made Daedalus a somewhat willing captive and a debtor to the king.

Daedalus's original home had been Athens, where he had earned his fame. A young nephew, Perdix, had been apprenticed to him there. The boy had proved himself to be as inventive as his master, a fact which pleased Daedalus not at all.

One day while walking along the seashore, Perdix had come upon the skeleton of a large fish. He picked it up, studied the backbone carefully, then carried it to his uncle's workshop. Once there, Perdix sought out a straight piece of iron. Next he proceeded to cut alternating rows of teeth along one edge of the iron. He attached a handle to one end and held up mankind's first saw to his proud gaze. The news of this invention spread rapidly, and people began to sing the praise of the young apprentice.

His next accomplishment was equally remarkable. Taking two pieces of iron, he fastened them in such a way that one remained fixed and standing, while the other could be moved around it. Thus did the first compass come into the world.

Now people began to say that the apprentice was greater than the master, and jealous rage seized the heart of Daedalus. He decided to rid himself of his nephew, who was too clever for his own good.

One afternoon as the two were sauntering about the city, Daedalus led Perdix to the top of a high tower. The boy went all unsuspecting, eagerly anticipating the fine view of the countryside which the height would grant them. Daedalus waited until Perdix's eyes were happily absorbing the beauties below them. Then, moving suddenly, he seized the lad and hurled him from the tower.

As he felt himself falling, Perdix screamed, and at once something marvelous happened. Where a moment before a frightened boy had been plummeting toward his death, suddenly a bird of bright plumage appeared and flew off on strong wings. Perdix had been changed into a partridge, a bird which has forever after shunned high places, making its nests in hedgerows and staying always close to the ground.

It was not long before Perdix was missed and Daedalus was questioned. He claimed to know nothing of the boy's whereabouts.

But doubt of Daedalus's innocence began to grow. Though he had tried to hide his jealousy, there were some who had suspected that he was resentful of his clever nephew. Ugly rumors began to spread about the marketplace, and Daedalus decided to flee Athens. He chose to go to Crete, taking his young son Icarus with him. Much to his relief, King Minos made them welcome.

At first Daedalus had enjoyed his exile. There had been the Labyrinth to build and the satisfaction of knowing what a high place he held in the king's esteem. But the years passed, and he grew bored with the limitations of life on an island. He grew tired of the same faces at court day after day. He wearied of hearing the same stories repeated night after night. More than anything else, there was nothing here to challenge his inventiveness. And he began to feel a prisoner, subject to the king's whims. He knew that Minos would never let him leave. He had to depart secretly, but land and sea were well guarded.

"Minos does not control the air," Daedalus told himself. "Therefore, I must find a way to fly from here."

He began to examine the wing structure of sea birds. He noted how they were curved, and how the smaller feathers fit over the larger ones. He decided to make two pairs of wings, one for Icarus and one for himself. To this end he began to gather feathers. He encouraged Icarus and his friends to gather feathers, too. People smiled at this sudden interest of the inventor and wondered what he might be up to. They felt sure that all in good time he would reveal to them some new wonder.

On the fateful night when Ariadne had sought his help, the two pairs of wings were ready, and Daedalus had determined to leave Crete on the morrow. Thus he would risk nothing by giving the princess the advice she sought. He knew that by the time Minos learned of the Athenians' escape (if they did escape) he, Daedalus, would be gone, as well.

Soon after sunrise next morning, while Theseus was sailing toward Naxos, Daedalus and Icarus, each carrying his pair of wings, stole from the palace and made their way toward a deserted stretch of shoreline. They walked for several miles, and the sun was high in the heavens before Daedalus said, "We have come far enough. Give me your wings that I may fit them to your arms."

With an excited, eager look, Icarus handed the wings to his father, then held his arms straight out from his shoulders. Carefully Daedalus fastened the wings. Next he put on his own, Icarus helping him with great patience.

The wing structures were beautifully fashioned. Taking the birds for his models, Daedalus had designed each wing with a slight curve. By means of wax and string, he had fitted smaller feathers over larger ones, keeping the whole as smooth and perfect as a swan's wing.

Smiling, he looked down at his son who stood on tiptoes, his great white wings extended, impatient to be off.

"Icarus, listen carefully. We will go to the edge of this cliff and there leap straight out into the air. I will go first and you will see how the air holds me up like a mighty hand beneath me." He paused and looked deep into his son's eyes.

Icarus returned the gaze steadily. "I'm not afraid, Father," he said. "I *want* to fly. I have been waiting for this day and moment."

"That is good," said Daedalus. "But remember, no tricks! Don't try to experiment. And above all, don't fly too high. If you do, the sun's fierce rays will melt the wax that holds one feather to another. I shall fly neither high nor low, but shall keep to the middle way; it is the easiest. And so must you."

Suddenly, there were tears in Daedalus's eyes and he stooped quickly and kissed his son. Then he was striding across the headland, the boy at his heels. He hesitated not a moment at the cliff's edge, but leaped forward, flinging his feathered arms wide. Icarus followed, and soon the soaring mortals were out over the sea, the island of Crete out of sight behind them.

For a while all went well. But as he became accustomed to the novelty of flight, a great daring seized

Icarus. It crowded from his mind all memory of his father's warnings, and he began to fly toward the sun. Up and ever up he went, exulting in his power. But then it happened as Daedalus had foretold it would. Under the sun's scorching rays, the wax of his wings softened and the feathers began to fall away. In a moment his arms were bare and he began plummeting toward the waters below him. For a few desperate moments, he beat the air with his naked arms. With a last cry, "Father," he struck the surface of the sea, and the waters closed above him.

Daedalus who had been looking back now and then to check the boy's flight, heard the cry. But when he turned his head the sky was empty behind him.

Suddenly Daedalus, swooping low, saw only a few feathers floating on the surface of the water. They told all. What Daedalus had feared had come to pass, and Icarus was drowned.

And that is why, since that time, those waters have been called the Icarian Sea.

Greatly sorrowing, Daedalus flew on until he came to Sicily, where the king made him welcome.

During these hours Minos had learned of Theseus's escape with the beloved Ariadne and his comrades. He knew there was only one person who could be responsible, and he sent at once for Daedalus. The messenger returned trembling in fear of the king's wrath and informed Minos that Daedalus and his son were both gone. But the king wasted no time in futile rage. Instead, he

put his wits to work and they served him well. At day's end he had thought of a way to discover the whereabouts of the inventor. Soon it was being announced in all the kingdoms of the known world that Minos, king of Crete, would give a prize of much gold to whoever was able to pass a fine thread through the many and intricate windings of a certain kind of spiral shell.

When the news reached Sicily, Daedalus secured such a shell, opened the closed end, and, tying a thread to an ant, put the insect into the shell. He then reclosed the end he had opened. Of course the ant had no choice but to search the shell for an opening by which it could escape. This it did, dragging the thread along with it as it explored each of the shell's spiral windings. When he decided it had reached the end of the shell, Daedalus freed it, showed the threaded shell, and claimed the prize.

When Minos learned that a man in Sicily had succeeded at the impossible task, he knew at once that Daedalus was that man. He immediately demanded that Daedalus be returned to Crete. But the king of Sicily refused to give him up. So, as he had so long ago against Athens, Minos declared war against Sicily.

This time, though, the gods deserted him. In the struggle that followed Minos was killed.

Daedalus lived on into old age, grieving for his son and repenting of the jealousy that had cost Perdix his humanity —and for which the gods had made him pay with the life of Icarus.

God of the Vine

THE BIRTH OF DIONYSUS

Cadmus, the man who killed the dragon, sowed its teeth, and reaped a harvest of warriors before founding the city of Thebes, had a daughter named Semele. Like a good many other mortal women, it was Semele's fate to have Zeus fall in love with her. In the form of a handsome mortal, he wooed her so persuasively that Semele consented, after learning who he really was, to marry him secretly. There was, of course, no other way Zeus could marry her.

Hera did not learn about this romance until some time after Semele had become the wife of the Father of Gods and was expecting his child. As usual, Hera's jealousy became a consuming flame, and she decided to rid the earth of her rival. Disguising herself as Semele's old

nurse and confidant, she appeared before the unsuspecting princess.

"My dear," said Hera in the old nurse's cracked voice,
"I have been thinking much of late about the secret you
have shared with me."

"That Zeus is the father of my child?" asked Semele,
smiling at the old woman's look of concern.

"Yes," answered the pretender. "Have you ever seen
him as anything but a mere mortal man? If he is truly a
god, and such an important god, then why does he not
assume his proper guise and glory? I suspect it is because
he *is* but a mortal man."

The girl looked thoughtful at these words. It was quite
true that she had never beheld her husband as a god. Always he appeared to her as a mortal, handsome beyond
most mortals, it was true; but still a mortal. How could
she be sure he was Zeus unless he showed her some proof?

The old woman's eyes never left Semele's face as these
thoughts went through her mind. Reading those
thoughts, the disguised Hera said, "I urge you, when
next he comes to you, to make him take an oath on the
river Styx to grant you a wish. When he has given the
oath, as he certainly will, then demand that he appear
before you in all his godlike glory."

"I will do that," promised Semele, and the old woman
shuffled off, a satisfied smile on her withered lips.

Not long after this, Zeus came to visit his latest love.
He had hardly greeted her, when Semele said, "I want

you to do me a special favor. Will you?" As she put the question, her smile was most bewitching.

"Dear Semele, ask anything you wish of me, and I swear by the river Styx, it shall be granted you."

This was the most solemn oath a god could take, and Semele knew he could not go back on it.

"Then if you be truly Zeus," she began, "show me . . ."

Guessing what her desire was, and knowing that no mortal could look upon the full radiance of Zeus without being destroyed by the sight, the god tried to stop her words before it was too late.

But, despite him, Semele blurted out, "Show me, if you be Zeus, your full godlike glory."

Sadly Zeus left her and returned to Olympus. There he arrayed himself in all his splendor. Brightness shone around him like the aureole of the sun, as fiercely dazzling, as fiercely consuming. Then, faithful to his promise, he returned to Semele. But when he entered her chamber, his blazing presence was more than her mortal flesh could endure, and she was consumed by it.

But just before poor, silly Semele could be entirely reduced to ashes, Zeus seized her unborn child from the flames and took it away with him. Eventually he gave the boy, Dionysus, into the care of Semele's sister, Ino. Dionysus was destined to become a god, though half mortal.

As god of the vine, he would bring much joy into the world—and an equal amount of sorrow.

PENTHEUS AND DIONYSUS

When Dionysus grew up, he became a wanderer upon the earth, traveling all over Greece and even into Asia. It was during these wanderings that he learned about the culture of the grape and how to change its juice into wine. Thus did he become god of the vine, or the god of wine. Now wine can make men gay and carefree, bringing them joy. It can also make them drunk and cruel. Thus some people worshiped Dionysus and others hated him, as we shall see.

Among those who hated him was Pentheus, king of Thebes. The mother of Pentheus was Agave, another daughter of Cadmus, and his father was Echion, one of the warriors who had sprung from the dragon's teeth. When Pentheus learned that Dionysus was returning from his far travels to his native city, he ordered the god seized. But the people, hearing of the god's approach, poured out of the city to meet him and do him honor. They surrounded their beloved god of the vine and would not let the guards of Pentheus near him. So the guards seized at random a man who was among those protecting the young god, and took him before the king.

"Wretch," roared Pentheus, "you have only a short time to live, for I mean to kill you as a warning to the people that I will not tolerate this worship of the god of the vine. Tell us your name, therefore, and why you are one of his followers."

"My name is Acetes and I am a man of the sea, a pilot."

Then Acetes told this strange story as King Pentheus listened closely.

One day piloting his ship toward Delos, Acetes put in at another island for fresh water. While he was climbing a hill there to test the wind, he saw his men coming toward him with a prisoner, a mere youth, graceful and fair of face. They had found him asleep and were planning to sell him into slavery. His beauty was so great, they thought he might be a king's son and so would bring a handsome price.

The youth showed no fear of his captors and looked upon their leader with smiling, confident eyes. Acetes, as he met the youth's gaze, felt there was something about him that was more than mortal.

"You had best let this lad go," he told his men. "There is that about him which persuades me that it will go ill with you if you do not set him free."

But the men would not listen to Acetes's advice.

"He was sleeping on the open ground like a common beggar with neither goods nor kin about him," declared one.

"We have found him and he is ours," cried another.

Acetes knew that if he pressed his point, the men would mutiny and seize the ship, making off with their captive and leaving their pilot helpless upon this island.

"Have it your own way, then," he said and shrugged. "But were it left to me, I should set the youth free."

Then he ordered everyone aboard the ship and they set sail. But hardly had they left the island when wondrous happenings began. A vine heavy with grapes began growing up the mast and all along the sides of the ship. There was the sound of music and the fragrance of wine. And as Acetes looked, wondering, at the young prisoner who stood leaning against the mast, he saw a crown of vine leaves suddenly encircle his head. It was plain that a god stood before him, and Acetes flung himself prone upon the deck.

At the same moment, the men of the crew were filled with a sudden madness. Perhaps it was terror. They began leaping overboard. As they reached the water, their bodies changed and took on the shape of dolphins leaping and playing beside the ship as if loath to leave it, as they have done ever since.

At last only Acetes was left aboard the ship with the young captive who was, of course, Dionysus, god of the vine.

Having heard the cries of his comrades as they knew themselves changed from human form, he had raised himself to his knees and faced the god, trembling with fear.

"Do not be afraid," said Dionysus. "You would have saved me and so now I will save you. Only take me to the island of Naxos and there leave me."

Acetes ended his story and waited for the king's next word. It was not slow in coming.

"A likely tale!" said Pentheus scornfully. "Take him away and put an end to his foolish life."

The guards seized Acetes and led him to a dungeon under the palace and shut the iron door upon him. But while they were making the preparations for his execution, the door opened mysteriously, the bonds fell from Acetes, and when the guards rushed to seize him, he was suddenly gone!

Now Pentheus decided that he, himself, would deal with the god, and leaving his palace he rushed forthwith to the wooded mountain where the worshipers of Dionysus were holding their revels, his own mother among them. When Agave beheld her son coming toward her through the wood, she shrieked, "See the wild boar. I will kill him with my own hands." The poor woman was under the spell of the god and could no longer command her wits. She rushed upon Pentheus. Other women, maddened like herself, followed her. And so terrible was their Dionysian frenzy that they fell upon the hapless king and tore him limb from limb.

Thus did the god of the vine avenge himself upon one who would deny him.

THE GOLDEN GIFT

During most of his wanderings, Dionysus was surrounded by a group of companions called satyrs. These curious creatures were part man and part goat, like the great god Pan. They were merry and full of pranks and mischief. But Dionysus's closest companion was an old man named Silenus. He was like a foster father to the young god, and his teacher.

Once when they were all trooping through Phrygia (where Baucis and Philemon had welcomed Zeus and Hermes), old Silenus became separated from Dionysus and the satyrs. Silenus, having drunk more wine than was good for him, crept into a shady glade, where he fell sound asleep near a pleasant fountain. It was there some servants of King Midas found him and straightway dragged him to the palace. Midas, who was a good-natured fellow, recognized Silenus and welcomed him with every honor. For eleven days there was feasting and merrymaking. But on the twelfth day, Midas had the old man returned to Dionysus. The god was so relieved to have his teacher returned to him safely that he said to Midas, "Ask anything you wish of me and it will be granted you."

A greedy look came into the king's eyes at these words and he said, "I wish that everything I touch may turn to gold."

"Your wish is granted," said Dionysus, smiling strangely.

Midas took leave of the god with hurried formality and hastened off toward his palace.

"I wonder if he really granted me the wish," he said and reached to touch the twig of an oak in his path.

Instantly the twig changed to pure gold, and Midas tore it from the limb and eagerly began making further test of the miracle that had been granted him. He picked up a stone; it became gold in his hand. A clod of earth also became shining metal. Midas was overjoyed. Gaining his own palace garden, he plucked an apple from its tree. It shone like the golden apples of the Hesperides in Atlas's garden at the edge of the western world. He it was who held the sky upon his shoulders.

As soon as Midas entered the palace, he ordered his servants to prepare a fine feast to celebrate his new-found wealth. But when the time came to eat, the king quickly realized the utter folly of his wish. He picked up a piece of bread. It turned to gold. He tried to cut the meat upon his plate, but his golden knife could not cut the golden food. He took up his wine cup, only to have it and the liquid it held changed to a shining solid. Two days went by, and Midas was torn by hunger and thirst. How he hated the gift of Dionysus!

At last he could bear his sufferings no longer. Raising his arms, he prayed to the god. "Save me from my own folly," he cried.

Dionysus heard his prayer and decided to grant it. After all, Midas had admitted his folly.

"There is a stream in Asia Minor," Dionysus told Midas. "It is called Pactolus. Follow it until you reach the spring from which it flows. Dip your whole body into that fountain, and your sin and its punishment will be washed away."

Midas did as Dionysus directed. He came to the stream and followed it until he reached its source. There he immersed himself in the cool water, and, as he did so, the golden power washed away from him and into the stream. Forever after its sands have gleamed golden.

A CROWN OF STARS

Dionysus was approaching Naxos on the ship hung about with vine leaves. Having routed Theseus with a dream, the god was coming to claim the abandoned Ariadne as his bride.

The ship bearing Theseus and his companions had not passed the headland of Naxos when Ariadne woke. For a moment she lay with closed eyes in that pleasant half-way state between waking and sleeping. Her dreams had been happy ones since they were of Theseus, and she wished them to continue. But, she sleepily reminded herself, Theseus was no dream lover. Waking would show him in the flesh, so waking was better than sleep. With this thought, she smiled and opened her eyes. Light showed beyond the trees above her. Stretching lazily, she glanced over to where Theseus had made his leafy bed. The bed was empty. Ariadne's smile widened. She had already noted the silence of the campsite, and now she knew that her hero and the others had departed with the dawn to hunt their breakfasts.

Ariadne sat up and began arranging her hair. She would wash her face at the spring nearby and be ready to greet Theseus on his return.

The way to the spring took her past the narrow cove where the ship lay beached. Ariadne turned her eyes in its direction and straightway her heart jarred so painfully within her breast that she sank to her knees. The ship was gone! With despairing eyes she searched the waters of the cove and beyond. Almost at once she saw the black-sailed ship slipping past the headland. A cry rose from her lips in which rage was mingled with sorrow. Why would Theseus abandon her thus? How could he be so false to the one who had saved him? Weeping wildly, she scrambled to her feet and sped down the beach. She waded into the water, her white arms held out in helpless appeal to the fast vanishing ship.

"Come back," she cried. "How can you leave me forsaken and alone on this island? What will become of me?

Oh, Theseus, though the gods have hardened your heart against me, do not leave me here to suffer until death releases me."

But the ship continued on its way, and in a little while was lost to sight.

Ariadne turned from the shore, and, slowly dragging her sandaled feet through the white sand, she made her way to the spring. Her silken gown, soaked with sea water, flapped clammily around her knees. In her frenzy she had torn at her hair, which now hung in disarray. Her lovely face was streaked with tears of anger and torment. Sorrow and bewilderment so gripped her she felt numb and wondered if she might be mad.

Walking thus dazedly, she came at last to the spring and knelt on its mossy rim. Dipping her hands into its crystal depths, she lifted the water to her face and the shock of its cold was comforting. Gradually her sobs ceased, and leaning back against a lichened stone she closed her eyes.

It was then, as she sat spent with grief, that the god of sleep mercifully appeared beside her. He held over her head a tree branch which had been dipped into the waters of Lethe, the river of forgetfulness, and Ariadne slept.

It was on this island of Naxos that Silenus and his troop of satyrs had remained after Dionysus had been taken captive from it. As Ariadne slept beside the spring, the satyrs came quietly out from their hiding places in the mountain cliffs and caves and began descending upon the coast. They knew their master was approaching on Acetes's ship, and they wanted to be ready to welcome him as he stepped ashore.

Slowly the vine-clad ship nosed into the cove following the same channel Theseus had sailed only hours ago. Dionysus stood in the prow smiling at the sight of his companions streaming down to the shore to greet him. The god leaped overboard and rode a wave to the beach, while the ship, as if moved by magic, turned and headed out to sea.

There was a noisy greeting as the satyrs welcomed their god back to his island. Then, alone, Dionysus started up from the shore. He knew who awaited him, and he knew where to find her. Arriving at the spring, Dionysus stood for a moment looking down upon the lovely girl who was to become his bride. Then he stooped and gently wakened her.

Ariadne opened her eyes, and for an instant they held a startled, almost frightened look. But the face of the man bending over her was so gentle and full of love that she smiled confidently at him. He reached his hand out to her, Ariadne laid hers in it, and the god pulled her to her feet. She looked around her like someone not quite awake.

"Where am I?" she asked. "This is no land I have ever seen before. And who are you who stands before me as handsome as a god with vine leaves in your hair?"

"Dear Ariadne," said Dionysus, "I am Dionysus, god

of the vine. And you have been left here on this island in order that you may become my bride."

Earlier that morning, when the god of sleep had appeared beside the spring to ease the heart of Ariadne, he had done more than merely grant her the boon of quiet slumber. So now she had no memory of anything that had happened before Dionysus wakened her. Looking upon the god, so tender and devoted in his attentions to her, she found it as easy to surrender her heart to him as she had her hand.

And so their wedding was celebrated on Naxos that very day, and the gods came down from Olympus to honor the marriage feast as they had the wedding of Harmonia and Cadmus so many years before.

Dionysus's gift to his bride was a crown of gold. But as the day ended, and the night sky filled with stars, he lifted the crown from her head and, giving it a fling, sent it into the heavens. As it traveled upward, the gold changed to stars, and when at last it came to rest against the sky, it glowed there as a crown of stars. Ariadne's crown became the constellation Corona, and she lives on forever in man's memory as Dionysus intended.

Not long after this, Dionysus obtained permission from Zeus to travel to the Land of the Dead and there claim his mother, Semele. Though she was mortal, she had given birth to a god, and so Zeus welcomed her to high Olympus where she would dwell forever among the Immortals.

Ariadne and Dionysus lived happily together for many years and had many children. And then one day they both simply vanished. Not even the gods knew where they had gone. But still men tend the vine as Dionysus taught them to do, and Ariadne's crown shines among the stars.

GLOSSARY

Acetes   a sē′tēz

Aegeus   ē′jŭs

Agenos   a jē′nor

Aeolus   ē′ō lŭs

Aethra   ēth′ra

Androgeos   an droj′ē us

Arcadia   ar kā′di a

Ares   ā′rēs

Argus   ar′gŭs

Ariadne   ar ĭ ăd′nē

Baucis   baw′sĭs

Cadmus   kăd′mŭs

Castalian   kăs tā′lĭ ăn

Caucasus   kaw′ka sŭs

Cercyon   sur′sĭ ōn

Corinth   kŏr′ĭnth

Daedalus   dē′da lŭs

Deucalion   du kā′lĭ ŏn

Dionysus   dī o nī′sŭs

Epimetheus   ep ĭ mē′thūs

Eros   ē′ros

Europa   ū rō′pa

Harmonia   har mō′ni a

Hephaetus   he fĕs′tŭs

Hera   hē′ra

Heracles   her′a klēz

Hermes   hŭr′mēz

Icarian   ī kar′ĭ ăn

Icarus   ĭk′a rŭs

Io   ī′ō

Labyrinth   lăb′i rĭnth

Lycaon   lī kā′ōn

Medea   me dē′a

Midas   mī′das

Minos   mī′nos

Minotaur   mĭn′ō tawr

Naxos   năk'sos

Nereids   nēr'e ĭds

Olympus   ō lĭm'pŭs

Pactolus   păc tō'lŭs

Pallas   păl'as

Pan   păn

Pandora   păn dō'ra

Parnassus   par năs'ŭs

Pentheus   pĕn'thūs

Phrygia   frĭj'ĭ ă

Perdix   pur'dĭks

Periphetes   per i fē'tēz

Philemon   fĭ lē'mŏn

Pittheus   pit'thūs

Procrustes   prō krŭs'tēz

Pyrrah   pir'a

Poseidon   pō sī'dŏn

Prometheus   prō mē'thūs

Sciron   sī'ron

Semele   sĕm'ĕ lē

Silenus   sī lē'nŭs

Styx   stĭks

Syrinx   sĭr'ĭngks

Themis   thē'mĭs

Theseus   thē'sūs

Thetis   thē'tĭs

Triton   trī'tŏn

Troezen   trē'zen

Zeus   zūs

ABOUT THE AUTHOR

DORIS GATES was born and grew up in California, not far from Carmel, where she now makes her home. She was for many years head of the Children's Department of the Fresno Free County Library in Fresno, California. Their new children's room, which was dedicated in 1969, is called the Doris Gates Room in her honor. It was at this library that she became well known as a storyteller, an activity she has continued through the years. The Greek myths—the fabulous tales of gods and heroes, of bravery and honor, of meanness and revenge—have always been among her favorite stories to tell.

After the publication of several of her books, Doris Gates gave up her library career to devote full time to writing books for children. Her many well-known books include *Little Vic, Sensible Kate, The Elderberry Bush,* and the Newbery Honor Book, *Blue Willow*.